FOR
THE
WIN

FOR
THE
WIN

How
GAME THINKING
Can Revolutionize
Your Business

KEVIN WERBACH
DAN HUNTER

DIGITAL PRESS
Philadelphia

Published by Wharton Digital Press
The Wharton School
University of Pennsylvania
3620 Locust Walk
2000 Steinberg Hall-Dietrich Hall
Philadelphia, PA 19104
Email: whartondigitalpress@wharton.upenn.edu
Website: wdp.wharton.upenn.edu

Ebook ISBN: 978-1-61363-022-8
Paperback ISBN: 978-1-61363-023-5

For Nate and Elena—DH

For Eli and Esther—KW

Contents

Introduction
Why Can't Business Be Fun?

An investment banker walks into his supervisor's office to announce he's jumping ship to a competitor. Sure, the firm paid him a hefty salary for the past five years, but one bank is the same as another, right?

A call-center worker reads the script on her computer screen in a measured tone. Her mind wanders as she struggles to get the customer off the phone. She tries to decide if she's too far behind on her daily call quota to take that next five-minute authorized bathroom break.

A mother wheels her shopping cart through the supermarket aisles, as her toddler becomes unruly in the child seat. She grabs products from the shelves, usually picking the cheapest one without much thought.

Disengaged, demotivated, disempowered, and disconnected. Isn't that how employees and customers always are—and always will be?

Now imagine a different set of scenarios. The banker basks in the status boost when his deal team tops the firm's internal leaderboard. The call-center worker feels rewarded—mentally and by her employer—when she helps a customer out of a jam. And the harried mother feels a jolt of pure joy when she realizes that next box of cereal means she has earned enough points to reach the next level on an online community site.

By at least some measures, the people in the first vignettes are doing their jobs effectively. Perhaps we want our leaders to be ruthless, our workers to be interchangeably efficient, and our consumers to be buying unthinkingly. But an exclusive focus on short-term factors will produce short-term benefits at best, while risking much larger long-term costs. These individuals are not engaged: They are phoning it in. It's hard to imagine any of the companies they interact with producing the next great innovation, viral hit product, or visionary CEO. And no one seems to be having much fun. But what's fun got to do with business, anyway?

A lot. For thousands of years, we've created things called games that tap the tremendous psychic power of fun. A well-designed game is a guided missile to the motivational heart of the human psyche. Applying the lessons that games can teach could revolutionize your business. The premise of this book is that fun is an extraordinarily valuable tool to address serious business pursuits like marketing, productivity enhancement, innovation, customer engagement, human resources, and sustainability. We are not talking about fun in the sense of fleeting enjoyment but the deep fun that comes from extended interaction with well-designed games.

Think about a time when you were engrossed in a game. For some of you it might have been golf; for others, chess or Scrabble; for others, FarmVille or World of Warcraft. Wouldn't you like to feel that same sense of accomplishment and flow in your work or to feel engaged and rewarded by your consumer interactions with companies? Organizations whose employees, communities, and customers are deeply engaged will outperform those that cannot engender authentic motivation. This is especially true in a world where competition is global and technology has radically lowered barriers to entry. Engagement is your competitive advantage. Game-design techniques provide your means to achieve it.

Games have been around as long as human civilization. Even videogames have a forty-year history and comprise a massive global industry that generates $70 billion per year. Hundreds of millions of people in every corner of the globe spend hundreds of billions of minutes every month playing console, PC, online, and mobile games. Games are popular in every demographic, gender, and age group, but they are especially pervasive among the generation now moving into the workforce.

Our starting question is this: What if you could reverse-engineer what makes games effective and graft it into a business environment? That's the premise of an emerging business practice called *gamification*. Our goal is to show you exactly how gamification can be used as a powerful asset for your organization.

One point to make clear at the outset: This isn't a book about videogames. It's not about the games industry, the gamer generation, the societal impact (good or bad) of game-playing, or how much the latest release of Madden Football cost to produce. It's not about 3D virtual worlds, advergames, or edutainment. It's not even about the internet or digital business. Sure, we'll talk about such things, but only as context. And because this is a business book, we haven't even mentioned the burning academic debates in games scholarship, such as the ludologists vs. the narratologists. (Don't ask.) No, this is a book about how you can use gamification to improve your business practices.

Gamification does not mean turning all business into a game, any more than innovation turns it into an R&D lab or Six Sigma turns it into a factory production line. Gamification is a powerful toolkit to apply to your existing business challenges, whatever the nature of your firm. Many of the best examples of game mechanics in business don't even look like games to those involved. The essence of games isn't entertainment . . . it's a fusion of human nature and skillful design. The hundreds of millions of people who flock to games on their computers, consoles, mobile phones, tablets, and social networks such as Facebook do so because those games were rigorously and skillfully designed, based on decades of real-world experience and research into human psychology.

Successful gamification involves two kinds of skills. It requires an understanding of game design, and it requires an understanding of business techniques. Few organizations are good at both. Knowing how to conduct a market segmentation or a minimum viable product analysis won't show you how to create enduringly engaging experiences. That's why most business managers find gamification so new and challenging. The reverse, however, is equally true. Expertise in programming, game-level design, art direction, or playtesting won't help you calculate the lifetime value of a customer, manage a team, or choose the right business strategy. In our research with companies and in teaching the world's first course on the business practice of gamification at Wharton, we see both the confusions and the insights that emerge when business practices and game design meet.

Underlying our effort is the recognition that traditional incentive structures to motivate customers and employees often fall short. The carrot and the stick don't cut it anymore; and money, status, and the threat of punishment only work up to a point. In a world of near-infinite choices, the old techniques are rapidly becoming less effective. Economists have been forced to acknowledge that people sometimes act in predictably irrational ways that frustrate basic tenets of management and marketing. How can firms use this knowledge to positive effect?

Research into human motivation gathered from scholarly literature demonstrates that people will feel motivated by well-designed game features. Monetary rewards aren't even necessary, because *the game itself is the reward.* Videogame players will, for example, invest enormous resources into acquiring virtual objects and achievements that have no tangible value. This is not to say that there isn't real money involved. World of Warcraft alone brings in nearly $2 billion per year. Zynga, which makes free-to-play social games on Facebook, generated $1.1 billion in revenue and nearly $200 million in profits in 2011, just four years after it was founded, largely from monetization of virtual goods.

Based on numbers such as these, a cottage industry is starting to trumpet the virtues of games and gamification. Several venture-funded startups now offer gamification toolkits to plug into your website or productivity tools such as customer relationship management systems. We're encouraged by this development, but we also want to sound a note of caution. It's easy to focus on the surface attributes of games and miss the deeper aspects. If gamification is just a gloss on existing marketing or management practices, or traditional rewards in shiny packages, it won't produce any added value. It could well make things worse. There's a reason most games fail: Game design is hard.

Whether you're an executive at a large corporation considering a gamification project, a staffer at a nonprofit seeking new ways to make a difference with your community, a student trying to understand the skills you'll need for job opportunities in a burgeoning field, or anything in between, our goal is to provide you with a pragmatic guidebook that includes all the basics you need to begin experimenting with gamification in your organization. Throughout, we attempt to provide you with a sophisticated understanding of the concepts around gamification, and we provide frameworks and step-by-step instructions to implement your ideas. Drawing on our research and conversations with executives, we reveal in *For the Win* how organizations of all types are putting gamification into practice. There are also numerous concepts drawn from academic scholarship in management, marketing, industrial organization, psychology, and other business fields. When the faddish aspects of gamification fade away, these well-grounded insights will remain valuable.

In emphasizing the practical focus of this book, we don't mean to give short shrift to the deeper implications of the techniques we describe. Gamification done right points toward a radical transformation in the conduct of business. If fun matters, it's because people matter. People matter as autonomous agents striving for fulfillment, not as black boxes or simplistic rational profit maximizers. Even as more of life is mediated through remote networked software systems executing programmed algorithms—in fact, because of it— the mysterious factors that make life meaningful should be a central concern of leaders. Recognizing the power of what we call "game thinking" is one step on that path.

Why We Wrote This Book

We both play videogames and have done so for much of our lives. If you play games long enough, eventually you start to notice things, like how people can't help but respond to game environments in playful and interesting ways. Even people who are smart, well-educated, and "shouldn't be wasting their time."

For years we were in a guild together in the multiplayer online game World of Warcraft. The guild was comprised of games designers and games researchers. The vast majority of them had PhDs or other advanced degrees, most had jobs at top universities or corporate research groups, and a high percentage had families. Not your typical bunch of teenagers seeking to escape reality. We watched with equal parts horror and amusement as these brilliant people got into fights over imaginary swords and worked together to defeat monsters that didn't really exist. This was unexpected and interesting, to say the least.

Then we took a look at our workplaces. In our day jobs, we teach in business and law schools. We began to think about the ways that arbitrary points-based systems—what we call "grades"—have a huge effect on students. The points and the grades aren't knowledge and learning; they are just the mechanisms that teachers create to assess and motivate students toward those important goals. There's nothing derogatory in the observation that education and work are really just games. We began to ask ourselves, why not make them better games?

We started to research gamification and taught the first business school course ever offered on the topic. We found that although there were great books on game design and on the speculative implication of games for society, there was nothing in print that gave a clear and rigorous explanation of how and why to build gamified systems. Most of what passed for "case studies" were anecdotal magazine articles or blog posts, and most of the "deep analysis" people pointed to was comprised of PowerPoint slides. We realized there was a real need for a research-grounded yet pragmatic guide that explained how to do gamification properly.

All of these experiences motivated us to write this book. But the real reason we wrote it has nothing to do with these very practical factors. We decided to write this book because gamification is fascinating, and it may turn out to be revolutionary. At its core, gamification is about finding the fun in the things that we have to do. Making business processes compelling by making them fun is about the coolest thing that we can think of. And we're only just starting to get a sense of how revolutionary this can be, in fields as wide-ranging as education, healthcare, marketing, relationship management, government, computer programming, and beyond.

Most of the concepts we'll discuss in this book are relevant in all of these contexts. Obviously gamification is going to be relevant for marketing departments that need to encourage consumer engagement with a product or to human resources teams that hope to motivate and engage employees. But it also applies in human resources management and in government and in social impact settings. Motivation is a magic ingredient in all these cases. A program funded by foundations to encourage low-income kids to read more at home isn't structurally all that different from one deployed by a consumer packaged goods manufacturer to sell more toothpaste. Both can become more effective through game thinking.

Of course, if you're the one managing the program, it makes a great deal of difference what you're responsible for. Our task is to show you the theory and practice of gamification and to demonstrate techniques and approaches that have been shown to work. From talking with the leading practitioners in the field, from teaching it, and from studying a large number of examples, we've identified what we believe are the critical elements for effective gamification. Your task is to pull from the gamification toolkits we'll outline in this book and mold something appropriate for you and your organization's specific needs.

A Map of the Territory

For the Win covers the concepts required to implement gamification successfully in any kind of organization. Like many games, it progresses through a series of levels. As you master each concept, you'll be prepared to take the next step.

At Level 1, you will gain a clear overview of gamification. At Level 2, we show you how to determine if gamification is going to work for your specific business problem. Here we teach you how to approach problems like a game designer. That means understanding exactly what a game is and the basics of game thinking. At Level 3, we get you to dig down into the motivations of the users of your gamification system and ask how gamification can better motivate them. Decades of research reveal surprising facts about the best ways to motivate behavior, which should inform any gamification project. We take a look at specific gamification techniques at Level 4, including the hierarchy of game dynamics, mechanics, and components.

At that point you will have the basics, but then it will be time to integrate them. At Level 5 we lay out how to put gamification to work through a six-step design process. At Level 6, we examine important risks, such as legal and ethical problems, oversimplistic approaches to implementation, and what happens when your players turn the tables on you.

If you're reading this book to learn more about what gamification is and how it works, you'll have a comprehensive foundation. If you're looking to implement gamification in your organization, you will be ready to experiment on your own or with a partner or team. Gamification isn't something you can expect to get right and leave unchanged for an extended period, because your players will demand more. Our goal is to put you ahead of the game. This book has everything you need to start. Additional resources are available on our website, http://www.gamifyforthewin.com.

Let the games begin.

A Note on the Title

"For the win," or FTW for short, is a gamer term believed to be derived from old-school TV game shows like *Hollywood Squares*, in which a player could win the game with a correct answer. It's used as an endorsement of a tool or practice that will lead to success in any context. As in: "Daily exercise FTW!" We find it an appropriate moniker. Gamification is a technique that businesses can use to be more successful. We hope you will use this book to help your business win in whatever ways you choose.

Getting into the Game
An Introduction to Gamification

> *Everything in the future online is going to
> look like a multiplayer game.*
> —Google chairman Eric Schmidt

Congratulations! You've begun! You're at Gamification Level 1.

*At this initial level, we explain why you should care about gamification,
and we answer some basic questions:*

- *Why are games valuable in serious business contexts?*
- *What is gamification?*
- *How can game concepts be employed in your business?*
- *When is gamification most effective?*

R oss Smith had a problem. His testing group at Microsoft plays a vitally important role for the software giant. Hundreds of millions of people use Microsoft Windows and Office daily. These software systems were built by hundreds of developers, modified repeatedly over a period of years, and customized for every major world language. Bugs and other errors are inevitable for such complex software systems. The testing group is responsible for ferreting them out.

It's a monumental task. Automated systems aren't sufficient, and the only way to ensure quality is for a vast number of eyeballs to review every feature, every usage case, and every dialog box in every language. It's not just the scale of the problem: Rigorously testing software is, much of the time, mind-numbingly boring. Even for a company with the resources of Microsoft, it's no easy matter to find enough people prepared to test products like Windows and Office. And the programs have to be tested in every language that Microsoft ships in. It's hard enough finding people to test in English, and ensuring that they do good work; imagine how hard it is confront the same problem in Polish, Urdu, and Tagalog.

If you were in Ross Smith's situation, you probably wouldn't think that fun was the answer to your problem. Software testing is serious business, with solemn financial and even legal implications for the company, and it calls for repetition and constant attention to detail. You might be surprised to learn, then, how Smith solved his problem: through games. Smith's group pioneered the concept of software-quality games that turned the testing process into an engaging, enjoyable experience for thousands of Microsoft employees.

For the Language Quality Game, Smith's group recruited Microsoft employees around the world to review Windows 7 dialog boxes in their spare time. They were awarded points for each suspicious bit of language they found and ranked on a leaderboard (a public "high score" list) based on their success. To ensure players didn't just click through screens without reading them, the organizers sprinkled in deliberate errors and obvious mistranslations. The game's scoring system tracked the performance of individuals and regions.

The Language Quality Game created a competitive dynamic for the participating employees. Employees wanted to win, and they wanted their languages to win. The Microsoft offices in Japan topped the regional leaderboard by taking a day off from other work to weed out localization errors. All told, 4,500 participants reviewed over half a million Windows 7 dialog boxes and logged 6,700 bug reports, resulting in hundreds of significant fixes. Not only did they do it above and beyond their work responsibilities, but a large number of them described the process as enjoyable and even addicting.

The Language Quality Game is not the only game developed at Microsoft to improve the quality of the company's products. PageHunt presents users with a webpage and challenges them to guess the queries that would produce that page. In playing the game, users generate large numbers of unusual connections—"JLo" for a page showing Jennifer Lopez, for example—that computers just can't generate by themselves and which radically improves the quality of Microsoft's Web search. The Code Review Game broke programmers into teams that competed against each other to win the most points for finding and fixing bugs in Microsoft products.

The Microsoft initiatives led by innovative managers like Smith are examples of a burgeoning set of new business techniques that leverage games for business benefits and which go by the name

Figure 1.1
Screenshot of a User Playing the Microsoft Language Quality Game in Hindi

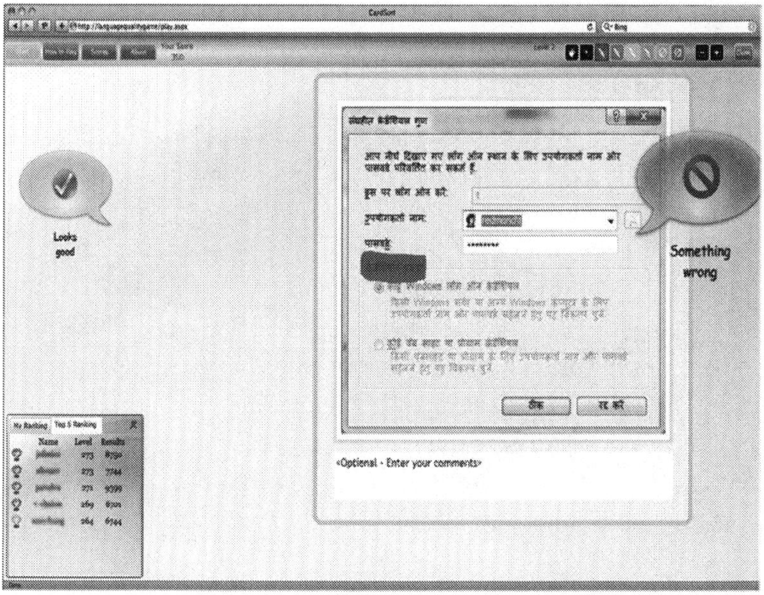

"gamification." These practices go beyond the game-based simulations that have crept into corporate training and related fields and instead involve the use of game techniques in all areas of business. They are coming soon to a business near you.

How Gamification Solves Business Problems

Ross Smith and the other executives we describe in this book have realized that the power of games extends beyond the objectives of the games themselves. A flight simulator can teach a pilot how to handle dangerous situations that might occur during landing. But if you're running an airline, you also care about whether your flight attendants exude a positive attitude, your baggage handlers do their best to get suitcases out on time, and your customers express loyalty. Gamification techniques can help companies improve every one of these mission-critical aspects of their business.

There are any number of settings in which this approach can work, but at this early stage three non-game contexts are particularly prominent: internal, external, and behavior change.

Internal Gamification

Ross Smith's initiatives are examples of *internal gamification*. In these scenarios, companies use gamification to improve productivity within the organization in order to foster innovation, enhance camaraderie, or otherwise derive positive business results through their own employees. Internal gamification is sometimes called enterprise gamification, but you don't have to be a large enterprise to use it. Even small companies and startups can apply game-design techniques to enhance productivity.

There are two distinguishing attributes of internal gamification. First, the players are already part of a defined community: the company. The company knows who they are, and they interact with each other on a regular basis. They may not have shared

Figure 1.2
Relationship between Different Gamification Categories

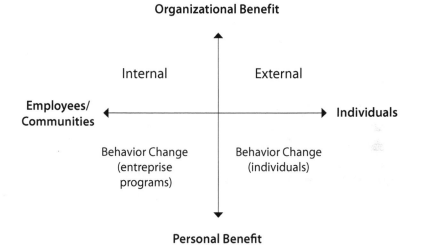

Organizational Benefit

Internal   External

Employees/
Communities ⟷ Individuals

Behavior Change   Behavior Change
(entreprise   (individuals)
programs)

Personal Benefit

affinities like the community of Harry Potter fans; in fact, they may be quite diverse in their perspectives and interests. However, they share reference points such as the corporate culture and desire for advancement and status within the organization. The Microsoft Language Quality Game worked because Microsoft offices around the world cared about besting their fellow Microsofties, and they had a shared commitment to shipping the best possible operating system.

The other aspect of internal gamification flows from the first. The motivational dynamics of gamification must interact with the firm's existing management and reward structures. The Language Quality Game was effective because its players weren't employed by Microsoft as localization testers. They participated in what Smith calls organizational citizenship behavior, not because their salaries depended on it. Internal gamification can work for core job requirements, but there must be some novel motivation. That could be the status of winning a coveted employee award or the opportunity to learn new skills.

External Gamification

External gamification involves your customers or prospective customers. These applications are generally driven by marketing objectives. Gamification here is a way to improve the relationships between businesses and customers, producing increased engagement, identification with the product, stronger loyalty, and ultimately higher revenues.

A good example is the *Record Searchlight*, a daily newspaper in Redding, California. Virtually every newspaper faces a quandary as readers shift from print to digital. The reporting, editorial, and investigative functions that newspapers provide depend on revenues from advertising and subscriptions, which largely evaporate when readers think they can get their news from blogs or wire service stories available online. Management at the *Record Searchlight* realized that it could combat this trend if it built a sustainable community on its advertising-supported website. The challenge was to turn passive readers into engaged users who would spend time interacting with multiple articles on the site and recommend them to friends.

To solve this problem, the *Record Searchlight* implemented a badge system for comments on its online articles. Users were rewarded with badges for particular numbers of insightful comments. A badge is just a distinctive icon that shows up on a user's profile when he or she reaches a defined set of requirements. That might not seem terribly important, but badges can be powerful motivators. They signify achievements and display them for all to see. Think about the patches used by the Boy Scouts, the insignias on military uniforms, or the "Harvard graduate" line on a resume. Gamified badges serve the same function digitally.

The paper's primary goal was to increase engagement with its website. After three months, the *Record Searchlight* saw a 10% rise in comment volume, and the time spent on the site increased by about 25% per session. Another goal was to improve the quality of conversations on the site. By encouraging readers to reward good comments by other readers, the badges reduced the number of offensive and problematic comments. That reduced editorial costs for the paper, and it made the online discussion area a more valuable tool for retaining readers.

As a form of marketing, external gamification can take advantage of all the sophistication of modern data-driven marketing practices. Gamification adds a richer toolkit to understand and stimulate customer motivation.

Behavior-Change Gamification

Finally, *behavior-change gamification* seeks to form beneficial new habits among a population. That can involve anything from encouraging people to make better health choices, such as eating better or working out more, to redesigning the classroom to make kids learn more while actually enjoying school, or building systems that help people save more money for retirement without lecturing them about how poor they're going to be in a few years' time. Generally, these new habits produce desirable societal outcomes: less obesity, lower medical expenses, a more effective educational system, better financial decisions. Behavior-change gamification programs are often run or sponsored by nonprofits and governments. However, they can also create private benefits.

Adam Bosworth is a long-time technology executive, having spent time at companies such as Microsoft, BEA Systems, and Google. He headed up Google's effort to develop electronic health records, which foundered amid operational and regulatory complexities. After building the deep technical foundations of several major software platforms, Bosworth was looking to do something that affected people more directly in a positive way. At the same time, like many technologists who spend a career sitting in cubicles, he wanted to get into better shape. He decided to launch a startup company that was still in the healthcare space but focused on motivating people to improve their personal wellness.

Keas, Bosworth's San Francisco-based startup, partners with enterprises to promote employee health and wellness. The company initially focused on presenting users with clear and compelling data about their health. If people could only see just how their choices about diet and exercise affected their bodies, they would be bound to respond. It didn't work out that way. No matter how compelling the data Keas presented, people couldn't get out of their established habits.

So Keas pivoted. It had already converted pages of health information into quizzes that tested users' health knowledge. Now, it incorporated those quizzes into a team-based game that included levels, strategy, and a leaderboard. The company wasn't sure users would go for this—who loves taking quizzes, after all? To be safe, though, it created what it thought were more quizzes than its users would ever get through during a twelve-week program.

The users plowed through them in a week.

That's when Bosworth knew he was on to something. Turning health and wellness into a game-like experience was the key to successful behavior change. Keas participant teams compete for rewards based on a combination of sustained real-world effort and learning how to be healthier. The results have been dramatic. At one hospital, employees using Keas collectively lost over 1,200 pounds, with 73% saying they felt more positive toward their employers and 64% saying they felt more productive at work.

Keas is a for-profit business, and its clients participate to cut down on their healthcare bills; but obviously there are major societal benefits when people make better health and wellness choices. Nonprofits such as Hope Lab are using gamification in similar ways to improve kids' health, especially in low-income communities. A White House initiative led by the Office of the National Coordinator for Health Information Technology and the Office of Science and Technology Policy is exploring games for health as a major national program. All of these efforts have in common the recognition that motivation is at the heart of sustained behavior change, and games are among the most powerful motivational tools.

The systems that Microsoft, the *Record Searchlight*, and Keas built look very different from one another, and they operate in different internal, external, and behavior-change contexts. But they are all examples of gamification and game thinking applied to particular business and social challenges.

Gamifi-what?

So what exactly is gamification? Companies have been applying game thinking to business challenges for some time without fully appreciating the scope of the concept. There are references to "gamifying" online systems as early as 1980. University of Essex professor Richard Bartle, a pioneer in multiplayer online games, says the word referred originally to "turning something not a game into a game."

The first use of gamification in its current sense apparently occurred in 2003, when Nick Pelling, a British game developer, established a short-lived consultancy to create game-like interfaces for electronic devices. The term fell into disuse, although during subsequent years, game designers like Amy Jo Kim, Nicole Lazzaro, Jane McGonigal, and Ben Sawyer, as well as researchers such as Ian Bogost, James Paul Gee, and Byron Reeves, began to talk about the serious potential of video games. It was only in 2010, however, that the term *gamification* became widely adopted in the sense that people use it now.

Even after major magazines have called it "the hot new business concept," using the word "gamification" often draws blank stares in conversations with executives. It's easily confused with terms such as "serious games" and "game theory." If you're looking for the mathematical models immortalized in the movie *A Beautiful Mind*, you're in the wrong place.

Gamification is a cumbersome word, and it doesn't capture the phenomenon in every respect. Many game developers and researchers worry—with good reason—that it trivializes the complexities of effective game design. Regardless, it's the term that has stuck. Eventually gamification may be called something else, but for now, we follow the common usage. The trouble is that there isn't a universally accepted definition of gamification. Our working definition is the following:

> **Gamification:** The use of game elements and
> game-design techniques in non-game contexts.

Let's break down this formulation and explain a little more about the three main aspects of the definition: game elements, game-design techniques, and non-game contexts.

Game Elements

A game manifests itself as an integrated experience, but it's built from many smaller pieces. We call those game elements. We'll go into more detail at Level 4, but for now, think of elements as a toolkit for building a game. Game elements for checkers, for example, include the pieces, the notion of capturing pieces by jumping, and turning a piece that reaches the last row of the board into a king. Notice that some of these are objects (the pieces), some are relationships among them (jumping), and some are abstract concepts embedding rules (making a king). In the Microsoft Language Quality Game, elements include the competition among international offices and the leaderboard allowing participants to compare their performance.

Just as you can assemble the same box of Legos into many kinds of objects, you can do different things with game elements. Most obviously, you can make a game. The game can be designed purely for fun (or associated revenue generation), or it can be designed to illustrate the complexities of the Israeli-Palestinian conflict. Or, you can assemble the elements into something that is not actually a game. When you're taking pieces of games and embedding them in business practices—challenging programmers to find bugs or having them guess search queries—then you're engaged in gamification, and the end product is, one hopes, a better and more compelling business practice.

You shouldn't forget that gamification isn't about building a full-fledged game. It's just about using some elements of games, and because it operates at the level of elements, using gamification offers more flexibility than using a game. When you're playing checkers, you can't mess around with the game elements. If you did, the game wouldn't be checkers, would it? With gamification, though, bending the rules is exactly what you're called upon to do. As the designer of a gamified system, you can and should tweak the elements to make the experience more engaging or to target certain business objectives. We'll talk about how you do this in later levels.

The key point is that game elements can be embedded into activities that are not themselves games. This radically expands the scope of opportunities. For example, the global consulting and auditing firm Deloitte realized that if it could only get more of its consultants to share information about their client meetings on the corporate intranet, it would promote more efficient knowledge sharing and collaboration across the organization. Mere exhortations were unlikely to move these busy professionals to invest the time. A simulation game wouldn't do the trick, either. Deloitte needed to motivate, not educate.

Deloitte's solution was to harness game elements by adding a feature called WhoWhatWhere to its internal social messaging platform. It encourages consultants to "check in" with details about their meetings. Leaderboards track who has checked in the most with a client or topic. The leaders gain recognition and social currency in the organization as experts, and this recognition motivates participation. WhoWhatWhere is an example of applying the best parts of games without actually creating one. That's what gamification is.

Game-Design Techniques

Gamification involves using game-design techniques, and this can be deceptively tricky. It's easy to believe that it is no great challenge to take a game element such as a point system and stick it onto a website: Want your customers to visit your website more often? Give them 100 points every time they check in! All it takes is a tiny bit of software code. And why not add a leaderboard? It's just a spreadsheet listing those points in rank order.

However, if you approach gamification in this way, you'll quickly run into trouble. What's the point of the points? Some users may find racking up a high score or topping the leaderboard inherently stimulating, at least for a while. But these users often get burnt out by the endless treadmill of points accumulation and abandon the system. And then there is the fact that most people don't find points particularly interesting. Many people look at the system and ask, "Why on earth should I care about this?" Even for the users who might care, the gamification design can be off-putting. New users may arrive with high hopes, only to abandon the system when they see the top of the leaderboard immensely far above them. These are just a few of the challenges you might encounter.

Even successful implementations can have missteps. As we mentioned, the Redding *Record Searchlight* is a good example of how external gamification can generate customer engagement benefits. At one point, though, the editors got carried away and implemented a "deal finder" badge for readers who signed up to receive promotional emails. It was a spectacular failure. Users of the gamified site found the emails so annoying that subscriptions to the promo list actually went down after the badge system was implemented.

How do you decide which game elements to put where, and how to you make the overall gamified experience greater than the sum of these parts? That's where game-design techniques come in. The aspects of games that make them fun, addicting, challenging, and emotionally resonant can't be reduced to a list of components or step-by-step instructions. Game design is a bit of science, a bit of art, and a lot of hard-won experience . . . just like strategic leadership, managing a team, or creating a killer marketing campaign.

Game design is hard. Even great game designers, like great film directors, sometimes produce poor-quality works. Successful companies such as Electronic Arts and Sony have spent tens of millions of dollars on online games that flopped. If you don't appreciate the accumulated knowledge and time-tested techniques of good game design, though, your chances of failure are far greater. That's why, in this book, we spend at least as much time on the "how" and "why" of gamification as the "what."

Non-Game Contexts

The final aspect of our definition is that gamification operates in non-game contexts. As noted earlier, this can mean internal, external, or behavior-change situations. The key element in each is that they involve real-world business or social impact goals. Your players are not storming a castle, they're exploring the website of your TV show. They're not killing dragons, they're collecting achievements on the way to improving their financial situation. This is important to keep in mind when designing a gamified system. Your players aren't there to escape from your product into a fantasy world; they are there to engage more deeply with your product or business or objective. Ross Smith's troops at Microsoft weren't hacking apart goblins; they were reading dialog boxes to find translation errors. Yet somehow, magically, it still *felt* like a game.

The challenge of gamification, therefore, is to take the elements that normally operate within the game universe and apply them effectively in the real world. In an array of situations, organizations are finding that gamification produces measurable results. Ross Smith's team at Microsoft showed that it could turn even a boring but valuable task into an exciting challenge.

Nike has done something similar with its Nike+ system, which uses wireless pedometers to feed data about their users' runs into an online service. Runners can visually track their progress, compare themselves with others, receive real-time encouragement from friends, and challenge each other to go the farthest or fastest. The system improves the experience of running and ties each pair of sneakers into an integrated environment that keeps customers returning to buy Nike shoes whenever their old ones wear out.

Taking Games Seriously

As a final point, we want to confront the question that's likely in your head or in the heads of those you discuss the concept with: *Why should a practice based on games be taken seriously in business?*

There are several good answers to this question. If you've bought this book and read this far, chances are you've already got a reason. Perhaps the notion of applying something as fun as games to something as potentially dull as work is inherently appealing. Perhaps your boss read one of those business magazine articles proclaiming gamification as an important trend. Perhaps you've seen a stimulating presentation from a gamification advocate. These are all legitimate reasons, but they rarely get to the essence of why gamification can be valuable.

We see three particularly compelling reasons why every business should at least consider gamification:
- Engagement
- Experimentation
- Results

Engagement

The most basic answer is that gamification is about engagement. The same human needs that drive engagement with games are present in both the workplace and the marketplace. Think of gamification as a means to design systems that motivate people to do things. Anything that makes your customers and employees want to strengthen their relationship with your company, or to buy your product, or to engage with the goals of the company, is going to be good for your business. The reason for this is simple. It turns out that our brains are wired to crave puzzle solving, feedback and reinforcement, and the many other experiences that games provide. Study after study has shown that games activate the brain's dopamine system, which is associated with pleasure. Neuroscientists have also found intriguing parallels between the brain's response to games and the process of inquiry. As renowned game designer Raph Koster writes: "With games, learning is the drug." What executive wouldn't want to harness the natural high that motivates learning and higher levels of engagement?

As we'll discuss, there's a danger in focusing too much on this pleasure-seeking reward dynamic as the basis for gamification. Just as drugs can make you happy for a while but eventually become counterproductive, gamification should draw on more than the brain's most primitive systems. A well-designed, nuanced gamification system can give you a powerful set of tools to develop challenges for your customers and employees that are meaningful and intrinsically engaging.

Engagement has business value in itself. Studies suggest roughly 70% of American workers aren't fully engaged in their jobs, and this undoubtedly affects not only their performance but their happiness. People know they should exercise more, eat better, get regular health checkups, use less energy, and so forth; the hard part is being sufficiently motivated to do so. And for consumers, engagement is what leads them to initiate a transaction. In some cases the benefits are indirect. Perhaps you want to engender camaraderie among your employees. Or maybe you want to convince a large number of strangers to tackle a collective problem, like studying NASA photographs to locate interesting new planets that automated systems can't find. Or identify your best customers, who have an outsized impact on your bottom line.

Experimentation

A second powerful aspect of game-based motivation is to open up the space of possibility. Mastering a game is all about experimentation. You expect to experience some failure, but because you can always start over, failure doesn't feel so daunting. In most videogames, you may win, but you can never permanently lose. If the game is effective—not too difficult, never too easy—players are continually motivated to strive for improvement. And they are encouraged to try new and different approaches, even crazy ones, to find better solutions. That ethos of constant innovation is perfectly suited for today's fast-moving business environment.

Table 1.1
Game Concepts in the Real World

Real-World Activity	Game Concept
Monthly sales competition	Challenge
Frequent flyer program tiers	Levels
Weight Watchers group	Team
Free coffee after ten purchases at Starbucks	Reward
American Express platinum card	Badge

Experimenting with the lessons in this book can pay dividends beyond gamification. As table 1.1 shows, game elements are already present in the real world. We just don't usually think about them in that way. News coverage of political campaigns and legislative battles often uses game language and imagery. Ask young people today how they see school, their relationship with brands, and their jobs, and they are quite likely to describe them in terms that sounds eerily game-like. The throwaway line that life, or work, is "just a game" rings strangely true.

The fact is that there's significant overlap between work, consumer interactions, and games. Sure, some people spend every moment of the workday waiting for it to end. Similarly, some coldly appraise their choice of products (such as cars) based on price, features, and gas mileage. Yet we've all heard of people who love their jobs and those who love their cars. If that doesn't sound strange, why resist the notion that games offer a pathway to improve experiences with business or social objectives?

Related to this, you may have come across "serious games" in your business or personal life. Chances are that the surgeon who operated on you and the pilot of your last flight trained with specialized 3D simulation games. There are substantial communities building games for health, military applications, environmental awareness, corporate training, and education, among other categories. There's even a remarkable public school in New York City, Quest to Learn, built entirely around games. In a slightly different vein, many games are designed to achieve marketing or advertising objectives, such as the annual Monopoly Game at McDonald's or the branded interactive games you'll often find on customer-facing business websites. Such advergames are now standard operating procedure for advertising and interactive agencies.

As we see things, serious games and their ilk are special cases of gamification. They are examples of using game design in non-game contexts by assembling game elements into full-blown games. There are substantial communities today around these practices, with their own books, conferences, and so forth. Some of our examples, such as the Language Quality Game, qualify as serious games, but most of them don't. Our primary focus in this book is on embedding game elements into existing practices, from exercise regimens to corporate innovation programs.

The rise of e-commerce, online communications tools in the workplace, mobile devices, and social media makes these experiences increasingly game-like. The similarities between the interfaces of Wall Street trading terminals, enterprise collaboration software, and massively multiplayer online games such as World of Warcraft are too striking to ignore.

Results

There's a final reason you should be interested in gamification: It works. Despite the novelty of the practice, a number of companies have seen significant positive results from incorporating game elements into their business processes. And not just exotic startups. Companies employing gamification include established giants such as Nike, American Express, Microsoft, and Samsung. They aren't doing so just because they think it's cool.

Game Thinking
Learning to Think Like a Game Designer

> *Someone says to me, "Show the children a game."*
> *I teach them gambling with dice, and the other says,*
> *"I didn't mean that sort of game."*
> —Ludwig Wittgenstein, *Philosophical Investigations*

At Level 1, we identified some situations in which gamification can make a difference in business, and we gave you some important definitions. Now, at Level 2, we explain the basic features of games and game thinking, so you can begin to recognize how to put game thinking to work in your projects and determine whether gamification can deliver the results you need.

We'll answer the following questions:

- *What is a game?*
- *How do I think like a game designer?*
- *Will gamification solve my business problem?*
- *How do I start?*

The world's deepest trashcan sits in a park in Sweden. It looks like any other trashcan, maybe four feet in height, painted blue like the bins around it. But when park visitors drop a piece of trash in it, they hear the whistling sound of an object falling for a very, very long distance, followed by a satisfying BONG as it hits the bottom. Candid videos of park visitors show them looking startled and confused initially, then smiling with delight at something so unexpected. Later videos show visitors ranging around the park grounds, looking for trash to drop into the can.

No enterprising Scandinavian elves dug a deep hole for the magical trashcan. Instead, a group of engineers created a simple motion detector and speaker system that they installed in the lid of a regular bin. Trash dropped in the bin actually falls about three feet, but the speakers mimic the sound of it falling hundreds of yards. The idea of this experiment was to answer a question: Would people drop more trash into a bin if it were fun? The answer is yes, indeed. The amount of trash deposited in the gamified trashcan was almost twice that of a regular park bin sitting nearby.

The trashcan was part of a Volkswagen initiative called The Fun Theory, which seeks to use fun to change people's behaviors. The Fun Theory also created bottle bank recyclers that look like slot machines; a lottery for drivers who don't speed, with a prize-pool from those who do; and most famously the Piano Staircase, featured in a YouTube video that has been seen over 17 million times.

We all know that using the stairs is good exercise, but most people prefer the comfort of an escalator. The Fun Theory turned the staircase at a Swedish subway station into a huge electronic piano, with each step corresponding to a key that made audible sounds. Result: 66% more people took the stairs. Those stair-climbers did something good for themselves, and they had a bit of fun in the process.

It shouldn't come as a surprise to see that fun motivates people. Gamification is the process of manipulating fun to serve real-world objectives. Fun, though, is a slippery concept. And asking, "Can we get people to do more of something by making it fun?" is much harder than defining fun in the abstract. The mind-set required to deploy fun in a considered and directed way is called game thinking. When both of us were in law school, we were often told that the objective of the program was to enable us to "think like a lawyer." Sure, we learned the hearsay rules of evidence, but the enduring takeaway was an analytical approach that could be applied in virtually any situation. Similarly, to be effective at gamification, you need to think a little like a game designer. If you do, you'll naturally focus on the topics we cover in this book. If you don't, you might use the right tools, but you'll probably generate poor results. Or you may not even know how to get from high-level concepts to real-world implementation.

Figure 2.1
The Fun Theory's Piano Staircase

To help begin thinking like a game designer, we start by asking an essential question . . .

What's in a Game?

First things first: we need to define what we mean by a game. You undoubtedly have an intuitive sense of the concept. Coming up with a precise definition, though, is surprisingly difficult. What unites Monopoly, cricket, Draw Something, duck duck goose, bridge, and Pac-Man?

You might think at first that fun is a necessary feature. But not all games seem like fun, nor is everything fun a game. So what about the typical features of games—teams, for instance? Well, not all games have teams. What about winning and losing? Well, not all games involve . . . you get the idea. It's almost impossible to define any essential attribute of games. The philosopher Ludwig Wittgenstein, whom we quoted at the beginning of this level, actually used the difficulty of adequately defining games to illustrate the indeterminacy of language.

Have no fear, that's the last you'll hear of Wittgenstein in this book. For business applications, all we need is a good enough understanding of games to be useful in developing real-world systems. One important aspect is that games are voluntary. No one can force you to have fun. As NYU divinity scholar James P. Carse said, "Whoever must play, cannot play." Second, games require those who play to make choices, and those choices have consequences that produce feedback. The choices may involve picking a weapon in a first-person shooter videogame or playing a particular word in Scrabble. Those decisions affect your experience playing the game. In fact, Sid Meier, legendary designer of the Civilization series of games, defines a game as simply "a series of meaningful choices."

Contingent choices highlight the connection between games and autonomy. Players feel a sense of control in games that is deeply empowering. We'll return to this concept in several places. Even more essential, though, is the fact that games seem somehow *different* from mundane reality. Even when the player is unambiguously sitting in an ordinary chair, in an ordinary office, doing an ordinary job, he or she can experience a pull that seems to originate somewhere else. That's what can make a gamified customer engagement system more effective than, say, a coupon, which doesn't change the nature of the underlying transaction.

To account for the otherworldly dimension of games, we ask your indulgence as we introduce one more philosopher.

The early twentieth-century Dutch thinker Johan Huizinga, in his classic book *Homo Ludens,* introduced the concept of the magic circle. The magic circle is a specially marked space that separates a game from the rest of the world. Players of a game step across this boundary into the magic circle, and by doing so voluntarily suspend the rules of the real world and accept the rules of the game. The boundary can be physical or virtual; what matters is that players accept that the game is real to them in some way. A game has some rules, and some objectives, and some obstacles to overcome in order to achieve those objectives; but the crucial element is the players' willingness to accept all those things and conform to them.

To state it briefly: A game is what happens in the magic circle.

Think of walking onto a gridiron to play football: By doing so you accept the risks of injury of a (legal) tackle by a defensive player. If someone wrestled you to the ground like Green Bay Packers linebacker Clay Matthews while you were walking down the street, you would sue him for assault and battery. Or consider checkers, where the object is to capture all your opponent's pieces. You could, of course, physically sweep all of your opponent's pieces onto the floor with the back of your hand. If you're playing checkers, you won't do that, because it would be cheating. And pointless. Whether it's checkers or football or Grand Theft Auto, the game is its own little immersive world.

Think of the power of the magic circle in a business context. You create a "world" to serve your strategic objectives . . . and it becomes meaningful to other people such as visitors to your website or staff in your call center. They are pulled toward the goals you've defined, not because you've forced them to be, but because they want to be. Doing this successfully is hard, and it comes with a set of responsibilities. The rest of this book is about all the complexities involved in effective gamification. The potential, though, is quite extraordinary.

If you're worried that building an effective game is an unfamiliar challenge requiring specialized skills, don't be. Gamification uses game thinking and elements but needn't involve creating an actual game. Most of your efforts are not going to involve a magic circle. Players may enjoy the challenge of a puzzle you create to encourage purchase of your product or collecting points on their way to better learning, but they won't permanently leave the reality that they're in. What you already know about your business and your customers will get you most of the way there. All you need are the tools and frameworks for more game-like experiences.

Game Thinking

Now that we've defined games, let's move on to game thinking. You need to learn to think like a game designer. This doesn't necessarily mean being a game designer. We're not asking you to build storyboards, 3D models, physics engines, or any of the things that go into modern videogames. And frankly, some examples of gamification are only game-like in the vaguest sense. Game thinking is a way to approach your existing management challenges in the same tradition as total quality management, process reengineering, design thinking, or any other business technique.

Compare game thinking to learning how to drive a car. You can read a book about what all the pedals and levers do, as well as the traffic rules in your jurisdiction. No matter how much studying you do, the first time you sit behind the wheel and turn the key, you'll feel uncomfortable and probably be a danger to those on the road around you.

There's a reason no one becomes a good driver without actually practicing driving, usually with an instructor in the car: Descriptions can never make you think like a driver. Knowing what appropriate acceleration feels like on the gas pedal, what to make of that car changing lanes in front of you, and whether to stop when the light turns yellow are bits of situated knowledge that experienced drivers internalize. In the same way, experienced game designers internalize a way of approaching problems that you may not be used to.

Game thinking means using all the resources you can muster to create an engaging experience that motivates desired behaviors. Some of the things that games do well include encouraging problem solving, sustaining interest from novice to expert to master, breaking down big challenges into manageable steps, promoting teamwork, giving players a sense of control, personalizing the experience to each participant, rewarding out-of-the-box thinking, reducing the fear of failure that inhibits innovative experimentation, supporting diverse interests and skillsets, and cultivating a confident, optimistic attitude. Game thinking takes advantage of such traits as a means to achieve business objectives.

Think of an objective you are facing. Let's say it's improving the retention of customers in your business. Maybe you want more clients to renew their insurance policies or you want more repeat buyers on your online fashion site. Traditional approaches might be to review your marketing campaigns, pricing practices, value propositions, or customer metrics. Game thinking asks a different question: Why do people buy your product or use your service in the first place? And it asks it in a particular way: What is their motivation? What makes them want to do business with you? Can you make it more compelling, more interesting, or more fun? Don't assume these factors aren't relevant because your business involves a bloodless exchange of money for value provided. Think back to our initial example of the world's deepest trashcan. The games designers of The Fun Theory took something incredibly boring—getting rid of trash—and transformed it. You can do the same thing in your business.

Notice that we're not asking you to think like a gamer. We already think like gamers because we all play games. For some of us the games have names, like Angry Birds or Red Dead Redemption; for others they are golf, Scrabble, or Texas Hold 'Em; and for others they are "acquire more Facebook friends" or "close enough deals to get that trip to Bermuda" or "ace the GMAT exam." When you're engaged in a game that you care about, you naturally try to succeed, whether that means vanquishing your rivals or earning the admiration of your friends. Evolution has wired our brains to be natural game-playing machines. That's very different from understanding what it takes to create an effective game experience. Applying gamification to solve business or other non-game problems puts you in the role of the game designer, not the game player. And that's not nearly as intuitive to most people.

In short, gamers try to win; game designers try to make gamers play. It's a subtle but important distinction. If you build an effective gamified system, your players—be they employees or customers or some other group—will attempt to hit the targets the game offers them. You, on the other hand, care about those targets only as a proxy for other things. Maybe you want your community members to reduce their carbon footprint, or maybe you want your consultants to share more information about clients with co-workers. Your baseline goal is to get your players playing and keep them playing. Only then can they generate the desired business benefits.

This is one reason why many videogames involve levels. Players start at Level 1 and pass through increasingly challenging stages as they progress. Reaching a new level is an accomplishment that gamers call "leveling up." Leveling up signifies progress and offers opportunities for encouraging feedback. To crib a phrase from former Apple CEO John Scully, it turns the journey itself into the reward.

Without levels, players may lose interest because they have no measurable sense of progress. Conversely, they may finish the game too quickly. Not all videogames have explicit levels, but they all have a sense of progression. Even "sandbox games," such as The Sims, that encourage players to explore a world with no predefined objectives still need dynamism and growth, either in the world or the player's mastery of the objectives. Otherwise they quickly become static, stagnant, and boring. Games are a process, not an outcome.

Notice here that we're using the word "players." We employ that term to refer to the participants in any gamified system, whether they happen to be your customers, your employees, your business partners, or your user community. Words matter. Just thinking about these groups as "players" can have salutary effects, for the same reason the department store giant Target studiously calls its customers "guests" and its employees "team members." Players are the center of a game, and they have a sense of being in control. After all, players pick the game; the game doesn't pick them. The excitement of the experience comes, as we've noted, partly from the players' sense of autonomy.

In a game, the sense of autonomy is always somewhat illusory. The game designer makes the rules and the game enforces them, especially in digital games, where so much happens through the software code that players never see. You can't build a condominium in Monopoly, even if you want to; you're limited to houses and hotels. That's true in business as well. Nike's customers can't design any shoe they want; they are limited to the choices Nike offers them. By offering more options for individual customization, though, Nike promotes a sense of empowerment. That's the secret to its successful NIKEiD offering, which lets buyers select personalized colors for every portion of the shoe. If you think of your customers, and even your employees, as players in a game you operate, you're more likely to identify such opportunities to give them meaningful choices.

Is Gamification Right for My Business Challenge?

Gamification isn't a solution to every business problem. Now that you've put yourself in the role of game designer, you should ask whether gamification makes sense for the challenges you hope to address.

Some things just aren't fun: A funeral parlor probably wouldn't want to gamify the buying process for a loved one's coffin. Equally important, though, some things are too much fun to gamify. You might play games such as three-legged races at the company picnic, but you probably wouldn't want to gamify the picnic itself. The picnic is an example of undirected play. Turning it into a structured process would do more harm than good. In other words, gamification works for contexts that are (or can be made) fun but which lend themselves to concrete business objectives.

Imagine that your local supermarket chain wants to implement gamification. It looks at its business and quickly concludes that some aspects are more amenable to gamification than others. It doesn't want the employees stocking produce to feel angry or dissatisfied with their jobs, but it's not clear how much its business would profit if those employees were super passionate. It may not be worth the investment to gamify this part of its business. On the other hand, engaged consumers are more likely to go out of their way to shop at their favorite store, producing direct financial benefits. Sales are one way of motivating customers, but they can be matched by competitors and cut into profits. A gamified system to increase the engagement and loyalty of regular supermarket shoppers makes a great deal of sense.

Let's define the process more systematically. To figure out where gamification might fit your needs, consider the following four core questions:

1. **Motivation:** Where would you derive value from encouraging behavior?

2. **Meaningful Choices:** Are your target activities sufficiently interesting?

3. **Structure:** Can the desired behaviors be modeled through a set of algorithms?

4. **Potential Conflicts:** Can the game avoid conflicts with existing motivational structures?

Motivation: Where Would You Derive Value from Encouraging Behavior?

Gamification is a form of motivational design, as we'll discuss in more detail later. It is fundamentally a means to get people interested in behaving a certain way. If your problem is a lack of qualified Java developers in your organization or that buyers consider your prices too high, gamification is unlikely to offer much in the way of solutions. Neither of these challenges can easily be solved with a more motivated population.

Generally, more engaged customers will purchase more, and more engaged workers will perform better, but the impact varies. A commodity product is unlikely to benefit significantly from gamification, because buyers typically choose these sorts of products on price alone. On the other hand, a company such as Apple, whose customers are already passionate, might find that game mechanics distract from the product itself or generate activity that doesn't produce additional revenue.

There are three main kinds of activities for which motivation is particularly important: creative work, mundane tasks, and behavior change. Some tasks involve emotional connections, unique skills, creativity, and teamwork. These are the high-value-added activities or customer relationships that make an outsized contribution to competitive advantage. They are also great candidates for gamification. Whether it's designing a new product or nurturing high-profile brand ambassadors, such tasks depend heavily on motivation. They work best when people are deeply engaged and focused, even passionate, about what they're doing. Gamification can give them a satisfying, individualized, ongoing rewarding experience unlike anything else.

At the other end of the spectrum are mundane tasks that involve adherence to defined procedures and that are purely individual in nature. Creativity isn't likely to be high on the list when one is hiring waiters and waitresses, for example. Gamification can also be effective in these situations, but it needs to be done differently. Your goal is not to trick people into tolerating a boring job; it's to help them find a measure of meaning in the activity. Take restaurant servers. A startup called Objective Logistics gamifies their work-scheduling process. The servers gain visibility into their performance beyond the tips in their pocket at the end of the night and are motivated both by recognition and the reward of more desirable shifts. Restaurants see average check size increase enough to improve profitability significantly.

Finally, there are behavior-change scenarios in which people understand something is good for them but have a hard time doing it. The challenge is to make the activity habitual. Practically Green is a Boston-based startup that promotes environmentally sustainable behavior among individuals and employees. It gamifies the process by assigning points, badges, and other game elements to specific activities, and by connecting participants to a supportive online community. Less than a year after launching, it has reduced over 14 million tons of carbon dioxide emissions, saved 25 million gallons of water, spurred recycling of 2 million pounds of garbage, and saved 6 million kilowatt hours of electricity.

Meaningful Choices: Are Your Target Activities Sufficiently Interesting?

Successful games require player autonomy, whether that's consumers deciding to purchase or workers deciding to take actions beyond their job requirements. Players can't just be following a predefined track. When they realize there's no inherent reason to care, any engagement bump they experience from game mechanics will be fleeting.

Meaningful choices simply mean options that give the player some freedom of choice, and noticeable consequences flowing from those decisions. In World of Warcraft, for example, a player can choose from several character classes, each of which has different strengths and weaknesses. Similarly, a Keas participant can engage in a variety of different health and wellness activities to earn points for her team. Even though all of these options serve the goals of the site, they give the user a sense of autonomy. A gamified system that offers rewards but no choices will quickly feel disempowering and boring for most players.

Structure: Can the Desired Behaviors Be Modeled Through a Set of Algorithms?

Games unleash the ineffable quality of fun, but gamification requires algorithms to measure and respond to actions. Also, it must be easy to record or track user activities, so the relevant data can feed into online systems that manage the game.

Consumer electronics giant Samsung has gamified its website with a program called Samsung Nation. Players can earn badges and level up by reviewing products, watching videos, and providing responses for product Q&As. Samsung built a point system that assigns values to all these actions. Sharing an action on Twitter is worth 100 points, while registering a Samsung product you just bought is worth 500. The 5-to-1 ratio is arbitrary, but it represents a rough estimate of the relative benefits to the network of the two activities. Similarly, Practically Green developed a proprietary metric for green actions such as reducing exposure to toxins and energy usage, which it promotes as an individual analogue to the LEED certification for environmentally sustainable buildings. Many gamified systems don't need specific point values of this type, but all require some way to model options algorithmically. If you have no structured way to assess, say, the difference between a high-quality proposed innovation and a poor one, gamification isn't likely to be a good means of motivating submissions to your corporate innovation process.

Potential Conflicts: Can the Game Avoid Conflicts with Existing Motivational Structures?

Studies show that game mechanics such as leaderboards can actually demotivate workers when the mechanic is entangled with traditional rewards such as salary and bonuses. When they see how low on the totem pole they are, many workers will give up. The climb up the ladder is too daunting. Others will internalize that the work is less important than the game and treat the work less seriously. Similarly, if your promise to customers is that you'll save them time and help them become more efficient, a gamified offering that encourages them to waste time in a seemingly frivolous activity may generate cognitive dissonance.

It's important to identify all the existing ways you motivate your target population, and to think through how they would function alongside gamification. Put yourself in the shoes of a player and ask what message your organization is sending. There isn't necessarily a conflict. For example, a startup called Recyclebank offers gamified rewards in many communities to encourage people to recycle. The prospect of receiving coupons doesn't automatically eliminate people's desire to recycle as a way to benefit the environment. However, Recyclebank has had to structure and position its game elements to avoid sending the message that recycling is purely a financial transaction.

Pulling It Together

You can think of the previous four questions as design goals. The ideal candidates for gamification are processes that depend on motivation, offer interesting challenges that are easily coded into rules, and reinforce existing reward systems. In reality, things don't always fall into place so nicely. The four questions are not either/or. In other words, the more meaningful choices, the better, and so forth.

Fill out table 2.2 for each business process or activity you are considering. Do this exercise before you think about what kinds of game elements or games you might use.

Table 2.2
Basic Gamification Checklist

	Players		Frameworks	
Activity	1. Motivation	2. Meaningful Choices	3. Structure	4. Potential Conflicts

For the hypothetical supermarket gamification initiative, the chart would look something like table 2.3 at the end of this level.

Before moving forward with your gamification project, you'll want to resolve each block of the chart in a positive way. In other words, you need a strong answer about why you meet each requirement or your project will be lacking in some crucial way. As your thinking evolves, go back and modify your answers. Then evaluate how changes in one box affect the others. You should do this before you make any decisions about the specifics of your system. It's much easier to make changes and avoid mistakes at this conceptual stage.

Table 2.3
Completed Checklist for Supermarket Example

	Players		Frameworks	
Activity	1. Motivation	2. Meaningful Choices	3. Structure	4. Potential Conflicts
Check-out clerk performance	Not clear that engagement would improve customer experience	Largely noncreative activity	Average time of customer checkout easy to measure	Perhaps intrinsic enjoyment can be added to a dull activity, but gamification might produce resentment
Shopper loyalty rewards	Give customers a reason to choose us other than price and in-store service, with direct revenue benefits	Let customers choose how to qualify for different kinds of rewards	Purchases automatically tracked through our POS system and loyalty cards	Customer and company interests aligned

Squares with an X indicate that the criterion does not support use of gamification for the activity. A partial X indicates that this criterion might support gamification, but is unlikely to do so.

LEVEL 3

Why Games Work
The Rules of Motivation

A soldier will fight long and hard
for a bit of colored ribbon.
—Napoleon Bonaparte

You've seen how gamification can work in general (Level 1), and
how to assess whether your business issue is amenable to gamification
(Level 2). Now we get to talk about your users and what makes them
tick. We'll ask:

- *What does research tell us about psychology and motivation?*
- *How can I make use of extrinsic and intrinsic motivators?*
- *How do I motivate behavior through gamification?*

Brian Wang and Richard Talens are in their midtwenties, usually dressed in t-shirts, and not very tan. In other words, they fit the stereotypes of hardcore gamers and Internet entrepreneurs . . . both of which they are. They are also impressively toned, and it's clear they spend a great deal of time at the gym. While at first this may seem incongruous, their penchant for working out is at the heart of what they do as gamers and startup founders.

Wang and Talens founded Fitocracy.com, a gamified website that tackles one of the hardest motivational challenges anywhere: getting people to exercise. Exercising is something most of us want to do but few of us actually do. We understand the benefits intellectually but have a hard time getting motivated.

Using various features normally found in videogames—things like levels, quests, badges, and points—Talens and Wang set about finding ways to motivate people to get up off their lounge chairs and into the gym. Fitocracy users are encouraged to track their jogging and their gym sessions, they are rewarded when they progress to a harder workout, and they share information, tips, and success stories on a social site.

Fitocracy knows its users. Some go for the feel-good stories alone, but there's a strong subgroup that responds best when its competitive

Figure 3.1
A "Duel" in Fitocracy

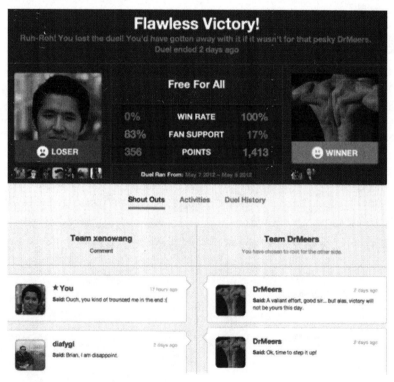

juices flow. So Fitocracy lets people challenge each other to virtual fitness duels, in categories such as "heaviest bench press" or "most distance run." Even there, though, it incorporates rooting sections that turn zero-sum battles into communal social experiences.

Fitocracy must be doing something right: the site went from 1,000 users to 200,000 in the space of a year, and Wang and Talens have collected numerous stories about users who have lost 100 pounds and turned their lives around. For Fitocracy, gamification is the key in moving users from merely wanting to exercise to actually doing it.

Whether it's promoting fitness, training employees to work more effectively, or encouraging customers to purchase stuff, managers regularly have to find ways to motivate people. Here at Level 3, we explore what makes people motivated to do things, so that you can start to think about what your users will enjoy and why they might do the things that you'd like them to do.

What Makes People Tick

The word "motivation" comes from the Latin *motivus*, meaning "serving to move." To be motivated is to be moved to do something. People are like objects: they have a certain inertia that needs to be overcome for them to move.

Let's say that you don't have any particular desire to see the latest Adam Sandler movie. Psychologists call that being "amotivated." It's not necessarily a comment on the movie; plenty of people pay $15 to go and watch it. So why do they go? Many reasons, of course, but a simple division is between those who *want* to see Adam Sandler clown around and those who feel like they *have* to go see him. *Wanting* to do something is called "intrinsic" motivation because, for the person involved, it lies inside the activity. On the other hand, feeling that you need to do something involves "extrinsic" motivation, because the motivation lies outside.

This may sound like an abstract distinction. After all, in both cases, you're going to see the movie. Yet it's critically important, and not just for gamification. Hundreds of peer-reviewed academic articles and scores of real-world case studies demonstrate that it matters tremendously whether intrinsic or extrinsic motivation is the basis for an activity. If you understand the difference, then you're halfway to understanding what types of mechanisms you can use to motivate your users. So what's the difference?

Imagine that you don't have any desire to go see Adam Sandler but your kids do, or your theater has a promotion offering free popcorn, or you see all of the cool kids you hope to impress walking into that movie. Along the same lines, you may not want to prepare the annual budget at work but it's your job, or you study for your statistics exam because you won't graduate without passing the class. These are extrinsic motivators. You are motivated to do something by reasons that come from outside your enjoyment or engagement with the activity: for your kids' benefit, because the cool kids are doing it, because it's a job requirement, or because you want to complete your degree.

We've all experienced extrinsic motivation. It's hard to overstate its importance in the business world and its literature. Many employees—perhaps most—turn up because they're being paid to do so or will lose their jobs if they don't. They may sometimes find enjoyment in doing a good job or mastering a task, but it's the exception rather than the rule. Cashiers at McDonald's are probably not asking "Do you want fries with that?" because it's fun. Salespeople work longer and harder because their end-of-year bonus is dependent on sales. Employees know if they get a bad performance review, they won't get promoted. Carrots and sticks are so common in employment that we tend to assume they are the only way to motivate behavior. Yet that's not the case.

Think about activities that you really, really want to do. You would do them without any hope of payment or other external benefits. Every person is different, but typical lists include socializing with friends, quality time with your spouse or family, playing sports, doing a job you love, eating and sleeping, reading, walking along a beach at sunset, or playing videogames.

Ask yourself *why* you want to do these things and you will find that there are lots of different reasons: being with and providing for your family is something that is part of your foundational sense of self as a person, eating and sleeping are needs you have as a human being, success in sports or work can promote feelings of competency and achievement, and walking along the beach and playing videogames are activities that are just plain fun. These are all intrinsically motivated activities.

Activities do not fall into these categories in and of themselves— there is no such thing as an amotivated task or an intrinsically motivated task. Motivation involves an interaction between a person and a task, in a situation and at a time. Remember the Adam Sandler movie example? You might have no strong feelings one way or the other about it. (You're amotivated.) Your neighbor, though, goes to see it because her husband promised her a fancy dinner afterward. (She's extrinsically motivated.) Her husband wants to go because he's a slapstick comedy aficionado. (He's intrinsically motivated.) Of course, some tasks are more likely to fall into one category or the other—taking out the trash is something that most people don't find intrinsically motivating—but in general motivation depends on how particular people relate to particular tasks.

What goes for Adam Sandler movies also goes for getting customers to buy, encouraging students, engaging workers, and any of the other objectives for a gamification project. In the following sections we pull apart the various features of intrinsic and extrinsic motivation, show how gamification can be used to motivate, and demonstrate some risks when gamification practitioners don't understand motivation.

The Rules of Motivation

Psychologists have been studying how to get people to do things for quite some time. In the second half of the twentieth century, the dominant theory was known as behaviorism. This approach sought to explain behavior purely based on external responses to stimuli. The best-known studies were done by Ivan Pavlov on his famous slavering dogs, and B. F. Skinner, who created the infamous "Skinner boxes" that gave food or electric shocks to pigeons and rats. Behaviorist studies like these examined the reinforcement effects of reward and punishment on animals and extrapolated the lessons to humans. The basic idea was that humans and animals responded to external stimuli in predictable ways.

Behaviorist thinking suggested that extrinsic motivation was the way to encourage people to do things. A reward or punishment, systematically applied, would condition and reinforce responses in anticipation of further rewards or punishments. Indeed, this is reflected in the standard business motivation methods of the era: the rewards of salary and bonuses and the punishments of demotion or firing. It was all very neat and industrial.

Against this behaviorist approach are a collection of "cognitivist" theories that ask what's actually going on in people's heads. Perhaps the most influential of these is the Self-Determination Theory (SDT) of Edward Deci, Richard Ryan, and their collaborators. Deci and Ryan suggest that human beings are inherently proactive, with a strong internal desire for growth, but that the external environment must support this; otherwise, these internal motivators will be thwarted. Rather than assuming, as the behaviorist approaches do, that people only respond to external reinforcements, SDT focuses on what human beings need to allow their innate growth and well-being tendencies to flourish.

SDT suggests that these needs fall into three categories: competence, relatedness, and autonomy. "Competence," or mastery, means being effective in dealing with the external environment: pulling off a difficult deal, learning how to dance the tango, filing a tax return. "Relatedness" involves social connection and the universal desire to interact with and be involved with family, friends, and others. It can also manifest itself as a desire for higher purpose, or "making a difference." And finally, "autonomy" is the innate need to feel in command of one's life and to be doing that which is meaningful and in harmony with one's values. Contrast the unhappiness you experience when you are forced to do something you don't want to do (or worse, that was contrary to your principles) against your feelings of joy when you are engaged in your favorite hobby or leading an important project at work.

Tasks that implicate one or more of these innate human needs will tend to be intrinsically motivated. In other words, people will do them for their own sake. Some examples are obvious: any hobby that you enjoy doing whenever you have a free moment, creative

Figure 3.2
Elements of Self-Determination Theory

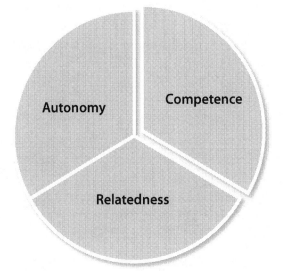

activity like writing or drawing, attending a dinner party with friends, solving a difficult crossword puzzle, taking a walk with no destination in mind, and so on. Others may not be: running a great meeting, giving a killer sales pitch, creatively helping a customer out of a jam, or performing a successful surgery.

In other words, intrinsic motivation can come into play in the workplace, even though there is already an extrinsic reward system of salary and promotion. The psychologist Mihaly Csikszentmihalyi found that people most commonly experienced the feeling of ultimate intrinsic motivation, which he labeled flow, on the job. Activities that address people's needs for competence, autonomy, and relatedness tend to be absorbing, interesting, and fun, regardless of the context. Think back to the Fitocracy duels. Participants choose the objectives of the competition and their opponents (autonomy); the mano-a-mano face-off creates a measuring stick (competence); and the rooting section loops in friends (relatedness). Players respond because Fitocracy activates all of the core SDT elements.

These motivators will manifest differently in each individual. Some players will be put off by the fear of losing a duel, which is why Fitocracy offers other mechanisms without head-to-head competition. Smart game designers, of course, realized this long ago. Popular videogames typically offer both player-vs.-player (PvP) and player-vs.-environment (PvE) challenges to address the two forms of competence. As one might expect, there are gender and age patterns here, but they aren't absolute. One of the authors, when playing World of Warcraft, loved nothing more than to sit in a secluded spot outside a major city to ambush passing players. The other put most of his energy into bloodlessly accumulating a huge fortune in the game's auction house. To each his own.

Daniel H. Pink's book *Drive* popularized the psychological literature on intrinsic motivation and demonstrated its significance to business. Create an environment in which your employees want to excel at their work, and you'll be much better off than if you rely exclusively on traditional levers like compensation. Several others, including management scholar Theresa Amabile, education reformer Alfie Kohn, and learning scholars Sandra Aamodt and Sam Wang, have demonstrated similar results in a variety of settings.

Games are perfect illustrations of the lessons of SDT. Why do people play? As we've already said, no one forces them to. Even a simple game like Sudoku activates intrinsic needs for autonomy (which puzzle I solve and how I solve it is entirely up to me), competence (I figured it out!), and relatedness (I can share the achievement with my friends). In the same way, gamification uses the three intrinsic motivators to generate powerful results. Levels and the accumulation of points can all be markers of competence or mastery. Giving players choices and a range of experiences as they progress feeds the desire for autonomy and agency. Social interactions such as Facebook sharing or badges you can display for friends respond to the human need for relatedness.

Although games would seem to be fun in and of themselves, they're not just about intrinsic motivation. Games may also involve extrinsic motivators. If you while away three blissful hours playing Call of Duty: Modern Warfare 3 on your Xbox 360, chances are you'll describe the experience as rewarding in itself. If you did so to beat your best friend's high score, or to win the cash prize in a tournament, or because your professor assigned it as homework, you might say something different. Each of these latter examples involves extrinsic motivation; and each of them is really powerful. As the designer of a gamified system, you'll have a series of choices about which motivational levers to pull, and how to do so.

The important distinction here is how the user feels about the experience, not the formulation of the reward. Consider three United Airlines Premier Executive frequent flyers. Juan is proud of being in such an exclusive club; he loves the feeling of walking on a red carpet past the hoi polloi at the gate. That stuff turns Alice off; she's just happy to have no carry-on bag fees and the ability to redeem miles for free trips. And all Esther cares about is access to the private airport lounges, where she can relax during those long layovers on business trips. Juan's craving for status is real, but it doesn't make that a good motivator for Alice or Esther. Each is motivated in different ways to achieve the reward.

Don't oversimplify the ways that game elements or gamified systems can produce motivational responses. And don't overgeneralize about how people respond to certain stimuli. Gamification is not just reward design. That sort of thinking is what led programming book author and game developer Kathy Sierra to label gamification "the high-fructose corn syrup of motivation." And she has a point. Many gamified sites and gamification platforms seem to assume that a virtual reward is inherently compelling. It's not. It might be a pale substitute for what people really want. Or as we describe in the next section, it might actually kill intrinsic motivation. Always focus on building authentic engagement; there are no shortcuts.

Lessons for Gamification

Now that we've described the basic framework for understanding motivation, what are the specific takeaways for successful gamification? The following lessons are sometimes counterintuitive, but they are well supported by studies and real-world examples.

Rewards Can Crowd Out Fun

Extrinsic rewards can be profoundly demotivating. Any gamification design has to take this into account. Sometimes giving people a bigger benefit to perform some activity will actually make them do it less, and worse. Alfie Kohn, the education reformer, published a book on this phenomenon in schools with the wonderful title *Punished by Rewards*. Psychologists generally refer to this as the "crowding-out" problem, because extrinsic motivators tend to crowd out intrinsic ones. For tasks that are interesting, intrinsic motivation dissipates when extrinsic rewards are tangible, expected, and contingent.

Consider how we learn to read. Many people find the pleasure of losing themselves in a book to be one of the true joys of life. It's one of the best examples of an intrinsically rewarding activity, at least when you read for the experience itself, not to achieve some other goal. But teaching kids to read can be an onerous task. Parents and teachers employ all manner of tricks to get them over the initial comprehension gap. Often these tricks fall on the more extrinsic side of the motivation continuum. It turns out that if you give kids tangible rewards like gold stars for doing well at reading—or, worse, if you give them money—they will improve up to a certain point and then stop. The tangible, expected, contingent reward initially motivates the kids, but its effectiveness plateaus dramatically. The effect is so obvious that it's become known by the grade level at which the extrinsic motivation loses its power: It's called the Fourth Grade Slump.

The crowding-out effect may sound counterintuitive, but when you think about it, there are good reasons for it. Paying a person to do something implies it's not inherently enjoyable, rewarding, or important. (Consider why we call salary "compensation.") It suggests the task is only worth doing to the minimal extent necessary for the reward. Before long, people begin to take the reward for granted. When the reward is expected, our mental arithmetic sees it as a kind of sunk benefit, providing increasingly little pleasure when it actually arrives. The task no longer seems intrinsically worthwhile, and the extrinsic rewards become increasingly poor substitutes.

Many research studies confirm that the crowding-out effect is real. Whether it's American children drawing pictures, Swiss citizens engaged in volunteer work, or Israeli parents showing up on time at day care, adding extrinsic rewards to intrinsically motivated tasks has been demonstrated to produce less effort and poorer-quality work. Moreover, the nature of the reward doesn't seem to matter. Virtually every type of expected reward (and punishment) that is contingent on performance will have the same effect: prize rewards, threats as punishment, deadlines, and centrally issued directives.

The lesson for gamification is simple: Don't mindlessly attach extrinsic motivators to activities that can be motivated using intrinsic regulators. Think back the Microsoft Language Quality Game. The reason the company didn't pay the participants for each dialogue box error they found, or even award a prize to the best individual or region, isn't that it wanted to save money. The fact that Ross Smith's group substantially improved the quality of Windows 7 localization at minimal cost was a positive feature but not the rationale for their approach. Money would have gotten in the way. The competition wasn't work; it was a fun challenge and a way to help the company produce better products. That's what made it so successful.

It's easy to get caught up in the ways the cornucopia of game elements listed in Level 4 can operate as extrinsic rewards. In part, this reflects the legacy of the loyalty program industry, which has spent the past few decades hooking us on frequent flyer miles and credit card reward points. Game thinking takes us beyond this limited view.

Boring Can Be Engaging

Extrinsic motivation is not always bad. Studies have found that it has a positive outcome on performance where the user is engaged in an otherwise amotivated task. In other words, extrinsic motivation helps people enjoy boring activities. Unlike the situation in which the task is intrinsically motivated, extrinsic rewards can encourage positive behavior and outcomes when one is dealing with dull, repetitive, and/or tedious activities. And we all know that everyone runs into those sometimes.

So extrinsic motivation isn't all bad. Let's be honest: There are many tasks that are deeply dull and will never be intrinsically enjoyable. Imagine you are trying to gamify tax preparation, estate planning, trash collection work, or the experience of undergoing an unpleasant but medically advisable procedure such as a colonoscopy. None of these tasks is something that people are likely to do because it's fun. You may have to use extrinsic rewards and punishments to change people's behavior. What if you're trying to do something like make math more fun for middle schoolers, nudge people to go to the gym, or encourage bank clients to understand the risks and rewards of financial products? In such cases there is the chance that you can apply intrinsic motivators, but extrinsic mechanisms may be necessary as a fallback.

LiveOps is a call-center outsourcing provider. Using a software platform, it has created a low-cost but high-quality virtual workforce of 20,000 Americans who answer or make calls part-time from home. It has successfully won business against offshore call centers by offering a better customer experience at comparable prices. A key asset for LiveOps is its ability to offer unemployed and underemployed Americans, including those with significant time limitations such as stay-at-home mothers, gainful employment and online skills development. Call-center work can be the epitome of drudgery, but many LiveOps agents describe their work in glowing terms.

Given its focus on creating positive experiences for its agents, LiveOps is a natural candidate for gamification. Indeed, the company has embraced gamification as a way to improve motivation. By adding relatively simple game elements—such as leaderboards and points—LiveOps was able to generate significant results. Service levels improved by about 10%, average time to handle a customer inquiry decreased by almost 15%, and sales performance improved significantly. The emphasis of LiveOps's gamification efforts is on learning and development rather than competition. Agents who level up or earn badges get the message that they are moving upward toward mastery of valuable skills.

There are numerous ways that you can use game mechanics to encourage certain types of behavior in tasks that can't be intrinsically motivated. A good example is in the traditional arena of marketing. Here, the experience of doing relatively mundane tasks with the promise of recognition or rewards to follow has been shown to be well

Figure 3.3
A LiveOps User Profile Page

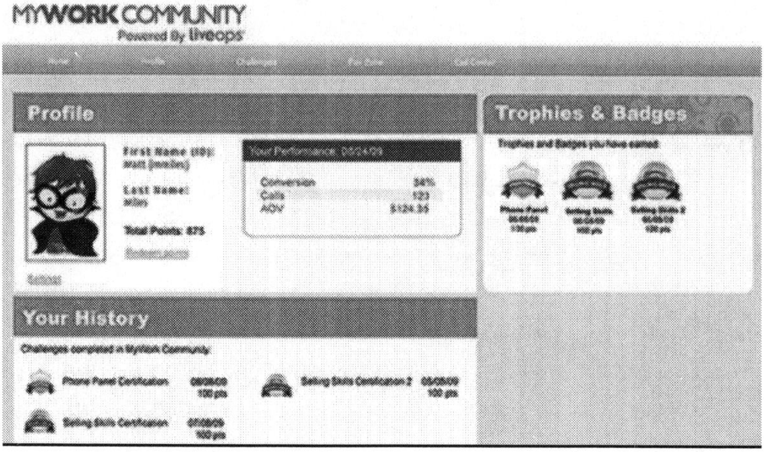

received by consumers. Rewards programs give purchasers points, tiers, and other psychological rewards in exchange for behaviors desired by program creators—usually the purchase of more product, or engaging with it in some way—and this has been shown to be an effective motivator of favorable activity.

The lesson for gamification: Extrinsic reward systems work for nonintrinsically engaging activities.

Tune Your Feedback

Feedback is trendy these days. Businesses and governments can now collect and display data to users in real time, and they are finding significant value in doing so. Police have shown a marked decrease in speeding when a driver is shown his or her speed on a display connected to a roadside radar detector. Drivers of hybrid vehicles use less gas when they're shown how accelerating and braking affects their mileage per gallon. Homeowners turn their thermostats down when given real-time feedback on what happens when they turn it up. Designed well, feedback loops push users toward desired behaviors.

Feedback in a gamified system can be the linchpin of effective motivation. Rypple, a Canadian startup, developed a service called Loops to provide performance feedback to employees. Rypple's first major client was a small social network provider you may have heard of: Facebook. Facebook's fast-growing workforce is overstocked with tech-savvy types who are highly attuned to social dynamics. Standard performance reviews, delivered top-down from a supervisor, didn't fit their mind-set. They wanted human resources to operate more like a game, in which players immediately see their score increase or their enemy's body explode when they perform a successful action.

Loops manages performance feedback from a number of sources, including input from co-workers, defined progress toward work goals, and coaching and validation from supervisors. Employees and teams can establish their own badges and "epic missions," defining the actions that mean something in the context of their workplace. Loops allows employees to monitor their performance constantly using this feedback. Rather than have one annual performance review, employees can see at any given time how they are doing against criteria that matter, and they can also see the recognition they've received. After several successful deployments, Rypple was acquired in 2011 by Salesforce.com, a large cloud services provider that is marketing its solution to a wider range of companies.

In building successful gamified systems, immediate and frequent feedback is necessary but not sufficient. Here are three important lessons about feedback:

1. Unexpected, informational feedback increases autonomy and self-reported intrinsic motivation. This has some concrete payoffs. It means that people enjoy being surprised by achievements and rewards that they didn't anticipate. Unlike the demotivating grind of contingent, expected rewards—for example, when you know that if you tweet 100 times about a product then you will get a "You Tweeted 100 Times About Our Product" badge—getting an unexpected badge or trophy stimulates positive feelings in the user. Players get a dopamine surge when it happens, a little like hitting a jackpot on a slot machine. This mechanism is called a variable reward schedule, and it's a well-established design pattern in game development.

2. Users like to get reinforcement about how they are doing. Informational feedback about progress toward a goal—"You've completed three out of the five steps necessary to unlock the AWESOME JOB badge," or providing some continuous graph of performance against specific metrics—will typically engage a player and may motivate him or her to complete the other steps necessary to complete the task. This is also something game designers have known for a long time. Videogames are veritable feedback fests, filled with scoreboards, flashing colors, musical fanfare, and more, whenever something important happens.

3. Users will regulate their own behavior based on which metrics are provided to them. If you provide feedback loops about customer satisfaction but not about sales figures, employees will begin to care more about customer satisfaction than monthly sales, and vice versa. Used wisely, this is a powerful tool in any gamified system—but bear in mind that all of the lessons and rules previously discussed still apply. If you create a feedback loop that works as an extrinsic motivator, you should expect that this may over time crowd out any intrinsic sense of satisfaction that the user might otherwise have experienced.

The lesson for gamification: Feedback loops regulate behavior in the direction of the feedback, and providing metrics for success will motivate the user in that direction.

Work Across the Motivational Continuum

Not all extrinsic motivation is experienced as completely outside the person. There is a difference between a student who is doing her statistics homework because she knows she will be punished by her parents if she doesn't do it and a student who is doing exactly the same homework because she wants to pass math so she can move on to the next grade, or because she's decided that she wants to be an economist and she recognizes that to do this she needs to learn stats. The first student experiences the motivation as unhappily external to herself, whereas the latter ones will experience the motivation as extrinsic but important in some way.

In other words, the latter students have begun to internalize the motivation within their set of values and sense of self. Deci and Ryan suggest that extrinsic motivation operates on a continuum between behavior regulators that are wholly external through what they call "introjected," "identified," and "integrated." Any task that would not be done except for motivations like rewards or punishments is generally perceived as external to the person. Tasks that are motivated by ego needs and thus marginally internalized—"I must do well at school"—are considered introjected. Tasks seen as important to one's future or values can be described as motivated by integration or identification.

A perfect example can be seen in online role-playing games that encourage the formation of tight-knit groups called guilds, which provide a system of mutual support for players within the guild. When they are part of the group, individual players cheerfully perform tasks that are remarkably dull—collecting materials or killing low-level monsters repeatedly to reach reputation thresholds—which they'd never do without the group. It's not that the task changes. It's that the user's need for relatedness dramatically changes the perceived nature of the motivation. The motivation becomes internalized as the user recognizes the value of the task to his guild.

The lesson here for any gamification design is significant: It is possible to design extrinsic motivators that are introjected, internalized, or integrated and so are more compelling to the user. Points and leaderboards are a good example: These gamification mechanisms can be seen as generating introjected behavior regulators because they appeal to a user's ego by allowing her to brag about her standing. Another example: Social gaming mechanisms allow users to become part of a larger community. This is likely to make them care more about the motivational device—whether that motivator is game element points, quests, badges, or some other mechanism. The motivator that was previously experienced as external to the user will begin to form part of the internal system of motivation, as the meaning of the community takes on greater value.

Don't Be Evil

Just because you can motivate someone to do something doesn't mean you should. One of our colleagues was asked to advise a large call-center operator on using game mechanics to increase productivity. He concluded that doing so would take an already awful work environment for the call-center agents and make it even worse. The gamification would be a tool for monitoring and dehumanizing the workers, not genuinely rewarding them. So he turned the job down. Gamification can motivate people to undertake activities that they otherwise wouldn't do. If that means hitting the gym regularly or having a more enjoyable engagement with a brand, it's a good thing. If it means your users are gambling away their paychecks at a casino or are being manipulated into taking valueless badges when they really wanted cash, it's more troublesome. Of course, not all call centers belong in the latter category: We gave an example in this level of one company, LiveOps, which takes a more enlightened approach.

In short, don't look at gamification as a covert tool to squeeze more out of customers, employees, or other groups. Look at it as a means to produce authentic happiness and to help people flourish while achieving your own goals at the same time.

LEVEL 4

The Gamification Toolkit
Game Elements

[I asked my three-year-old daughter what she was made of.] She paused to consider. She looked down at her hands, turning them over, and studying them. And then, brightly, she announced: "I'm made of skin!"
—Jesse Schell, *The Art of Game Design*

Now that you have earned your way to Level 4, you know how to think about your problem in gamification terms, you understand how to motivate your users, and you have seen how to implement a basic gamification system. It's time to level up to some more advanced features of game thinking so that you can deliver the most compelling implementation. We'll ask:

- *What are points, badges, and leaderboards (PBLs), and why are they so common in gamification?*
- *How do games actually work?*
- *What are game elements and how can we apply them?*

Club Psych, launched in 2010, is a gamified website built around USA Network's successful TV program *Psych*. It offers users an array of challenges, such as watching a video, answering a trivia quiz, and joining the show's fan club. A mystery game called Hashtag Killer allows players to simulate interactions with the show's characters over Twitter and Facebook. The mobile app Psych Vision lets fans unlock prizes and chat with each other while watching the show on TV. All of these actions earn points that can be redeemed for virtual goods or physical merchandise, up to unique items such as posters signed by the show's cast. Items are frequently added and occasionally removed to stimulate continued interest.

The most obvious surface-level gamification features of Club Psych are points, badges, and leaderboards (PBLs). Points are accumulated for undertaking challenges and can be redeemed for rewards; and they are shown in a leaderboard to compare how the player is doing to other players. Players pick up badges for all manner of achievements undertaken on the site.

Club Psych employs PBLs effectively: After the introduction of the gamified site, overall traffic on the USA Network site increased 30%, online merchandise sales increased nearly 50%, and pageviews for the official *Psych* website increased 130%. Club Psych's users are undoubtedly more engaged than the average couch potato. And they have shared *Psych* content over 300,000 times on Facebook, reaching 40 million Facebook users. Considering that *Psych* only has about 4.5 million regular viewers, that's a tremendous amount of publicity for the show. Hashtag Killer was even nominated for an Emmy Award.

Does this mean that effective gamification is about adding points, badges, and leaderboards to your business process and calling it a day? Well, not exactly. Although PBLs are incredibly common in gamification, they're not the whole story. And sometimes they can be damaging to what you want to do. Jesse Schell, the noted games designer and Carnegie Mellon University professor quoted in this level, tells the story about his daughter's idea that she's made of skin to make the point that a surface-level understanding of the human body is fine for a three-year-old but not so great if you're a physician. The same is true of gamification. In this level we'll start with PBLs, the "skin-deep" gamification features, and then we'll work deeper into the body of gamification to explain other approaches that you'll want to consider using.

Figure 4.1
Club Psych

The PBL Triad

In our research, we've examined well over 100 implementations of gamification. Many of these systems—if not the vast majority of them—start with the same three elements: points, badges, and leaderboards. As we noted, Club Psych is no exception. PBLs are so common within gamification that they are often described as though they are gamification. They're not, but they're a good place to start.

Used right, PBLs are powerful, practical, and relevant. They can also be used in significantly more sophisticated ways than one might imagine. On the other hand, PBLs have important limitations.

So they're the obvious place to start building your gamification toolkit. You can't build a successful gamification system without understanding their up- and downsides.

Points

We often see points used to encourage people to do things by collecting them. The assumption is that people will buy more widgets or will work harder in exchange for points. This is a simple approach that occasionally works to motivate those people who like collecting things ("Look at how many points I just received!") or for those who like competing against others ("No one else has 1,000,000 points!")

But points can be used in many other ways, and we need to understand how the humble point can serve many functions. We've identified six different ways that points are used in gamification:

1. **Points effectively keep score.** This is the typical way they are used in gamification systems. Points tell the player how well he or she is doing. Someone who has earned 32,768 points has been playing longer or more successfully than someone with 24,813 points. Points can also demarcate levels. For example, "You need 10,000 points to reach Level 5, at which point you unlock the 'super player' achievement and get access to new content." In this case points represent the true "play space" of a game because they define progress from the beginning of the game to its objectives.

2. **Points may determine the win state of a gamified process, assuming it has one.** Sometimes you will want to use points to create a win condition: if you want to give away a prize, say.

3. **Points create a connection between progression in the game and extrinsic rewards.** Many gamified systems offer some

real-world prizes for reaching certain levels or for redeeming virtual points: 1,000 points gets you a set of steak knives and 1,000,000 points gets you a round-trip ticket to Tahiti. Club Psych takes this approach, but it's common in all manner of marketing and promotional devices that have been used for years.

4. **Points provide feedback.** Explicit and frequent feedback is a key element in most good game design, and points provide feedback quickly and easily. Points are among the most granular of feedback mechanisms. Each point gives the user a tiny bit of feedback, saying that he or she is doing well and progressing in the game.

5. **Points can be an external display of progress.** In a multiplayer game, or in an environment in which members of the community or workplace can see each other's scores, points show others how you are doing. That can be significant as a marker of status.

6. **Points provide data for the game designer.** The points that users earn can easily be tracked and stored. This allows the designer to analyze important metrics about the system. For example, how fast are users progressing through the content? Do they seem to be falling off or stalling out at certain junctures?

By understanding the nature of points, you can use them in ways that meet the objectives of your gamified system. Do you want to encourage competition? Then use points as scores. Do you want your users to be hooked by the dopamine drip of constant feedback? Then use points to give them a sense of mastery and progression, without showing them how others are doing. And so on.

Bear in mind that points are very limited. They are uniform, abstract, interchangeable, and well, pointlike. To put it another way, a point is a point. Each additional point simply indicates a greater magnitude, and nothing more. This is one reason why badges are often found in conjunction with points systems.

Badges

Badges are a chunkier version of points. A badge is a visual representation of some achievement within the gamified process. (The terms "badges" and "achievements" are often used synonymously in gamification.) Some badges simply demarcate a certain level of points. Fitbit is a gamified system that allows people to use a wireless pedometer to track the number of miles they walk or run. The system displays a badge when the user exceeds certain point thresholds, such as 50 miles in a week or 10,000 steps in a day.

Figure 4.2
Fitbit Badges

Other badges signify different kinds of activities. Foursquare, a service that engages users with local businesses by encouraging them to check in to a location with their cellphone, has numerous badges for all manner of achievements. Users unlock the "Adventurer" badge as soon as they check into ten places registered with the Foursquare system, and they receive the "Crunked" badge for checking into four bars in one night. (No one said that badges need to be socially responsible.)

Researchers Judd Antin and Elizabeth Churchill suggest that a well-designed badge system has five motivational characteristics:

1. Badges can provide a goal for users to strive toward, which has been shown to have positive effects on motivation.

2. Badges provide guidance as to what is possible within the system and generate a kind of shorthand of what the system is supposed to do. This is an important feature for "onboarding," or getting the user engaged with the system.

3. Badges are a signal of what a user cares about and what he or she has performed. They are a kind of visual marker of a user's reputation, and users will often acquire badges to try to show others what they're capable of.

4. Badges operate as virtual status symbols and affirmations of the personal journey of the user through the gamification system.

5. Badges function as tribal markers. A user who has some of the same badges as other users will feel a sense of identity with that group, and a clever gamification design can connect the badges with a system of group identification.

One of the most important attributes of badges is their flexibility. Many different kinds of badges can be awarded for many different kinds of activity, and the range of badges is limited only by the imagination of the gamification designer and the needs of the business. This allows the gamified service to engage a more diverse group of users and to appeal to their interests in ways that a single points system cannot. Your friend may have a completely different set of badges than you, even though you're both playing the same game. Nonetheless, both you and your friend will, one hopes, find the badges meaningful and interesting.

Badges can serve a credentialing function. Remember the Good Housekeeping Seal? It tells consumers that the product in question passed tests by *Good Housekeeping* magazine. That means you didn't have to trust the product; you just had to trust *Good Housekeeping*. One of the nice things about badges as credentials is that they are infinitely flexible. You can receive a badge for anything, from the silly to the serious. Some organizations are even looking to badges as a foundation for new forms of online education and training. This isn't as crazy as it might first sound: A diploma from an elite university is a kind of badge that holds out the promise of a certain level of skill and achievement on the part of the diploma holder.

In internal gamification contexts, credentialing badges can be a way for your employees to demonstrate certain skills. Every large enterprise has extensive corporate training programs, and employees participate in more training outside the firm. Badge systems are useful in this context.

Leaderboards

Leaderboards are the final leg of the PBL triad, and perhaps the most troublesome. On one hand, players often want to know where they stand relative to their peers. A leaderboard gives context to progression in a way the points or badges can't. If performance in the game matters, the leaderboard makes that performance public for all to see. In the right situation, leaderboards can be powerful motivators. Knowing that it's just a few more points to move up a slot or even to emerge on top can be a strong push for users.

On the other hand, leaderboards can be powerfully demotivating. If you see exactly how far you are behind the top players, it can cause you to check out and stop trying. Leaderboards can also reduce the richness of a game to a zero-sum struggle for supremacy, which inherently turns off some people and makes others behave in less desirable ways. Several studies have shown that introducing a leaderboard alone in a business environment will usually reduce performance rather than enhance it.

There are various ways to make leaderboards work for your gamified system. A leaderboard need not be a static scoreboard, and it need not only track one attribute. In gamification, leaderboards can track any feature or features the designer wants to emphasize. There's nothing wrong with multiple leaderboards measuring different things or leaderboards that aren't universal for all participants. Leaderboards can also be tied to social networks to provide more contextual, and less troubling, information about how players are faring.

PBLs as a Starting Point

Taken together, the PBL triad forms a useful starting point for gamification efforts. In our gamification courses for Wharton MBA students, almost every student team incorporated PBLs into their gamification design, despite our admonitions to consider alternatives. There's just something comfortable about these components, and they make sense in lots of projects. Related to this, turnkey gamification products from vendors such as Badgeville, BigDoor, and Bunchball almost always incorporate these three elements as standard features. It's therefore easy to implement these three approaches using off-the-shelf products. And PBLs link gamification to well-known enterprise features like loyalty programs, reputation systems, and employee competitions.

As valuable as they are, relying just on PBLs can get you into trouble. PBLs aren't right for every project, and they're not the only features that you can deploy in a gamified system. If you want to extract the maximum value from gamification, you'll want to move beyond PBLs. This is where we head next, where we start to think a little more about what makes a game and what makes a game work.

Braving the Elements

We've already seen a number of gamification features that are not PBLs, in examples like the teams in the Language Quality Game or the duels in Fitocracy. It turns out that PBLs are special cases of what we will call "game elements"—that is, specific characteristics of games that you can apply in gamification.

To build a house, you need to understand small-scale components such as hammers and nails and 2x4s; midlevel concepts such as framing, plumbing, and blueprints; and high-level abstractions such as master bathrooms, structural engineering, movement flow, and aesthetics. Each of those is an element of house construction. The sum total of the elements and the ways they are put together is the house itself. Designers and builders go from a vacant lot to a finished house using such elements. Executives in charge of gamification design understand games in a similar way and can use this understanding to build, pull apart, and rebuild their projects.

There are three categories of game elements that are relevant to gamification: dynamics, mechanics, and components. They are organized in decreasing order of abstraction. Each mechanic is tied to one or more dynamics, and each component is tied to one or more higher-level elements.

Dynamics

At the highest level of abstraction are dynamics. The most important game dynamics are:

1. Constraints (limitations or forced trade-offs)
2. Emotions (curiosity, competitiveness, frustration, happiness)
3. Narrative (a consistent, ongoing storyline)
4. Progression (the player's growth and development)
5. Relationships (social interactions generating feelings of camaraderie, status, altruism)

Dynamics are the big-picture aspects of the gamified system that you have to consider and manage but which you can never directly enter into the game. Analogies in the management world would be employee development, creating an innovation culture, or pretty much any other large-scale objective you'll find in an airport book on business. The dynamics in Club Psych include high-level features like the way that the prizes relate to the narrative in the television series (for example, bobblehead dolls of the actors and the recurring appearance of a pineapple) or the relationships formed when users are able to comment on the latest episode.

There's an important point here. Good business leaders and managers create desired dynamics in their organizations. They rarely, if ever, have the opportunity to sit outside the business and design it from scratch. Rather, they have to push an existing organization in the right direction through hiring and promotion, management practices, leading by example, and so forth. When creating a gamified system, on the other hand, you can play God. You're the designer. The way to think outside the box in gamification is to build a better box.

Mechanics

Mechanics are the basic processes that drive the action forward and generate player engagement. We can identify ten important game mechanics:

1. Challenges (puzzles or other tasks that require effort to solve)
2. Chance (elements of randomness)
3. Competition (one player or group wins, and the other loses)
4. Cooperation (players must work together to achieve a shared goal)
5. Feedback (information about how the player is doing)
6. Resource Acquisition (obtaining useful or collectible items)
7. Rewards (benefits for some action or achievement)
8. Transactions (trading between players, directly or through intermediaries)
9. Turns (sequential participation by alternating players)
10. Win States (objectives that makes one player or group the winner—draw and loss states are related concepts)

Each mechanic is a way of achieving one or more of the dynamics described. A random event, such as an award that pops up without warning, may stimulate players' sense of fun and curiosity. It might also be a way of getting new participants hooked (onboarding) or keeping experienced players involved (interest curves). In Club Psych there are mechanics that involve social challenges, like watching preview clips with your friends, and rewards that range from virtual goods to rare merchandise.

Components

Components are more-specific forms that mechanics or dynamics can take. The fifteen important game components are:

1. Achievements (defined objectives)
2. Avatars (visual representations of a player's character)
3. Badges (visual representations of achievements)
4. Boss Fights (especially hard challenges at the culmination of a level)
5. Collections (sets of items or badges to accumulate)
6. Combat (a defined battle, typically short-lived)
7. Content Unlocking (aspects available only when players reach objectives)
8. Gifting (opportunities to share resources with others)
9. Leaderboards (visual displays of player progression and achievement)
10. Levels (defined steps in player progression)
11. Points (numerical representations of game progression)
12. Quests (predefined challenges with objectives and rewards)
13. Social Graphs (representation of players' social network within the game)
14. Teams (defined groups of players working together for a common goal)
15. Virtual Goods (game assets with perceived or real-money value)

Just as each mechanic ties to one or more dynamics, each component ties to one or more higher-level elements. Services such as Club Psych use points and badges extensively to connect player actions to the higher level mechanics and dynamics. Thus, players working on puzzles that relate to the current episode may earn 100 points, answering challenges, receiving feedback, moving closer to rewards, and connecting to the narrative context of the television series. Or if they reach high-enough levels, they can collect limited-availability badges that are themed from the *Psych* series (resource acquisition, rewards, narrative, progression, constraints).

Notice that our previous triad of points, badges, and leaderboards can be found in this grouping. PBLs are particular components that may be used in gamification. As we've stressed, they are only a few of the possible components, which may not be the best for your context. One reason to review the pyramid of elements is to recognize the variety of options for a gamification design.

Integration

We've given you a lot of information about game elements in fairly general terms. It may not all feel coherent right away. We've provided quick sketches of different sorts of game elements so that you understand that there are lots of features you can use, and so that you have some ideas to try out. In the next level, we'll show you how to use the design process to apply these elements. But you should now have a sense that all of the game elements exist in a hierarchy, as shown in figure 4.3.

Putting all these elements together is the central task of gamification design, and having knowledge of these game elements will make your gamification project compelling. Bear in mind, though, that no gamification project will include all of these elements. In fact, it's unlikely you would ever utilize all the items within any one category. However, if you haven't considered a large set of possible options at some stage of your design process, your gamification

Figure 4.3
The Game Element Hierarchy

Dynamics
are the big-picture
aspects of the gamified
system that you have to
consider and manage but
which can never directly enter
into the game.

Mechanics
are the basic processes that drive the
action forward and generate player engagement.

Components
are the specific instantiations of mechanics and dynamics.

project will suffer. As we move up to the next level, you'll see how to integrate these elements into the gamification design process.

One final caveat: Having a list of elements is necessary but by no means sufficient. Creating a successful new service is always harder than deconstructing an existing one. In particular, building an engaging gamified service takes more than checking off the right boxes. You need to ensure that the elements match the particular demands of your situation. And you need to implement them well. Facebook and MySpace are social networking sites with similar basic capabilities, but one made billions and the other cratered after its acquisition.

Muscles and Bones

When we first looked at the example of Club Psych, we saw the surface of the system but not the organs that lay underneath the skin. PBLs form the most obvious features of gamified systems such as Club Psych, but they may not be right for your task. And although you now have an understanding of the elements that constitute games— the bones and the muscles, if you will—that you can apply to your process, it may be hard to understand how you can harness them in a meaningful way. How, then, do you go about putting everything together? We tackle this question in the next level.

Game Changer
Six Steps to Gamification

Games are the most elevated form of investigation.
—Albert Einstein

This is where we bring all of our learning together. We now have all the building blocks to make gamification work. At Level 5, we see how to make it happen, by looking at:

- *Gamification as a design process*
- *Six steps to implement gamification effectively*
- *Techniques to apply high-level concepts to specific projects*

Now that you know the essential concepts of gamification and game thinking, it's time to use them. This has to be done in a thoughtful way. If your process boils down to brainstorming what might be fun for your players and picking the game elements that seem to work, there's a good chance you'll fail. Whether you are going to create, plan, execute, and assess a gamification project yourself or leave the implementation to outside service providers, you're going to need a process to make the project work.

Gamification requires a fusion of art and science. On one hand, it involves emotional concepts such as fun, play, and user experiences. On the other hand, it's about engineering measureable and sustainable systems to serve concrete business objectives. Creative types tend to focus on the experience and give short shrift to metrics. The quants and MBAs, on the other hand, can lose sight of the big picture amid their spreadsheets.

Fortunately, there's a discipline that bridges this gap: It's called design. A good design process melds creativity and structure to match people's needs with technical feasibility and business realities. Whole books have been written on design thinking in business. Here we offer a design framework that is customized for developing gamified systems.

Gamification is best implemented in six steps, each of which starts—like the word "design"—with the letter D:

1. DEFINE business objectives

2. DELINEATE target behaviors

3. DESCRIBE your players

4. DEVISE activity cycles

5. DON'T forget the fun!

6. DEPLOY the appropriate tools

You will see that only in the last step, do we talk about gamification components like leaderboards and badges. That's deliberate. The mechanisms of gamification look really easy, especially today with so many plug-and-play tools readily available. If anything, they are too easy. The fact that you can add points to your website with a few lines of code and white-label software-as-a-service doesn't mean that you should. Designing how to map the available techniques onto your particular situation is what's difficult, which is why we spend the first five steps focusing on these issues.

1. Define Your Business Objectives

You already started to do this in Level 1, but it's time to make things absolutely concrete. For effective gamification, it's critical to have a well-developed understanding of your goals. That might sound obvious, but it's easily overlooked. We're not talking here about your overall organizational mission, whether expressed in terms of profitability, shareholder value, mission statement, or otherwise. We mean the specific performance goals for your gamified system, such as increasing customer retention, building brand loyalty, or improving employee productivity. If you don't start with this step, your gamification project may get off the ground, but it will probably fail eventually.

DevHub is a small business website-building tool that looked to increase engagement using gamification. Using Foursquare as a model, DevHub's founders figured that game elements could overcome the fatigue that kept most users from implementing all the functions the site offered. They added experience points, levels, and virtual currency that could be redeemed for additional content and features. Next, they relaunched DevHub's website-building service as an empire-building game, complete with a stable of cartoon characters called Devatars that appeared on users' sites when they completed tasks. The percentage of users completing site-building activities increased eightfold. Even better, virtual goods became a new revenue stream, representing almost 30% of DevHub's revenues after the relaunch.

A great gamification success story, right? Wrong.

At that point, DevHub only attracted about 10,000 active users. The numbers may have looked good on a percentage basis, but the reality was that the virtual goods brought in only about forty cents per user per month. Enticing users to complete tasks didn't help with DevHub's real problem: attracting large numbers of users and monetizing their actions. It may have even hurt, by alienating potential customers who found the space empire game silly. DevHub had to lay off staff and search for a new business model. (It eventually made a successful pivot into a white-label website-development tool for small-business directory services.)

The lesson from DevHub is that gamification, even when effective, can produce results that don't necessarily help. To avoid this pitfall, your first step is to make a list of all potential objectives. Make each goal as precise as possible, but the initial list can be expansive because you'll winnow it down. Perhaps you want to attract high school dropouts from low-income communities to use your personal finance educational tool, or perhaps you want your employees to suggest out-of-the-box ideas for new business opportunities. Then rank the list in terms of importance. You may need to trade off lesser goals for more significant ones, at least initially.

Now, go through your list and cross off anything that is a means rather than an end. In other words, it's really only a stepping-stone to a more important goal. Getting users to accumulate points and badges isn't a reason to implement a gamified system; it's something that happens within one. Having large numbers of players visit your website is only an end if it's directly valuable to you; otherwise it might generate support costs without concomitant revenues. A good test is whether—if something you list were the only result from your gamification project—you'd be satisfied it was a success. As a final check, add another column, and, next to each objective, explain how it would benefit your organization.

As you work through your design and development process, keep coming back to this goal list. Even if your priorities change, it will keep you grounded and focused on what really matters.

Figure 5.1
The Objective Definition Process

2. Delineate Your Target Behaviors

Once you've identified why you're gamifying, focus on what you want your players to do and how you'll measure them. Behaviors and metrics are best considered together. Target behaviors should be concrete and specific, for example:

- Sign up for an account on your website.

- Post a comment on a discussion board.

- Exercise for at least 30 minutes.

- Share information about your service on Twitter.

- Comment or vote on suggestions by others.

- Visit your restaurant.

- Buy Bounty paper towels.

The behaviors you are looking for should promote the ultimate business objectives you previously defined, though the relationship may be indirect.

For example, getting users to spend more time on your site or to talk about your products on Facebook doesn't translate immediately to revenue, but it may still be desirable. Come up with as many possible behaviors as you can. You don't want the system to be too complex or confusing, but you want to give users a range of options and activities to pursue based on their preferences.

Once you've listed all the desired behaviors, develop your metrics for success. These are the ways you translate behaviors into quantifiable results. Gamification runs on software algorithms. Behind the scenes, it translates activities into numbers and uses those numbers to generate feedback. The numbers might or might not be transparent to the player. They might see a shower of sparks and an announcement they've reached the "grand poobah" level or unlocked the "hungry hippo" achievement. In designing the system, however, you need to decide precisely what those mean.

As we discussed earlier in Level 4, points are an easy way to quantify and measure any kind of progress. Whether or not your gamified system will present the user with points, you'll probably use it internally to define the relative values of behaviors in your design process. The value of the points should correspond to your best estimate to the relative value of the activities to your organization. For example, you might decide that reading a discussion post is worth 1 point, whereas commenting on it is worth 5 points, and posting is worth 10. You'll quite likely find that you need to tweak these point values once you start testing your system. Do the best you can at the outset, and be prepared to revise.

"Win states" form a second kind of success metric. Of course, everyone likes to win, and so it seems like a no-brainer to include some kind of "win" for your users. However, from a design standpoint, winning is problematic. It means that some players haven't won, and this may turn them off. And for those who do win, it means that the game, or that part of the game, is over. That's not good if your goal is to get them to keep coming back. Remember, your goal isn't to sell a game, it's to use game elements to achieve some organizational objective. You can get around these limitations to some degree by creating localized or temporal win states. Perhaps every week there's a new contest, or "winning" just means an achievement. Foursquare added levels to many of its badges when it realized its single state badges created an all-or-nothing dynamic rather than encouraging continued progression.

Analytics are the algorithms and data used to measure key performance indicators for your gamified system. Every online activity generates an event that can be tracked and measured. E-commerce and social games companies have become adept at learning how to aggregate data from large numbers of user transactions to measure the success of their services. Common analytics include the ratio of daily to monthly active users (an indication of how often users return), "virality" (how likely users are to refer their friends to the service), and the total volume of points awarded or virtual goods purchased. The right things to measure will depend on your context; an enterprise gamification project will likely involve analytics that are different from those of a marketing project, for example. Don't forget to identify whether existing monitoring systems within your organization are tracking the same behaviors.

3. Describe Your Players

There will be real people using your system. Who are they? What is their relationship to you? Employees, for example, aren't in the same situation as customers. How much does their relationship with you involve others?

What might motivate your players? That question probably won't have an easy answer, but put yourself in their shoes and identify as many possible motivations as you can. The discussion of intrinsic and extrinsic motivation at Level 3 should give you a good foundation to decide which motivators can most effectively be addressed through your gamified system. Don't forget to think about what demotivates your players. In other words, what makes them less likely to complete a relevant task: Is it volition (a perceived lack of desire) or faculty (a perceived lack of capability)? The former calls for an engagement-oriented approach, while the latter calls for progression systems that gently walk the player up the difficulty curve.

Remember that not all users are the same. You'll want to segment your players so that your system is appropriate for more than one subgroup. Segmentation is a common practice in marketing and human resources. It's even more important here. Because games and gamified systems typically offer choices to the player, you don't need to choose a single segment to target. There are World of Warcraft players who do nothing but engage in player-to-player combat and others who spend all of their time exploring the world through solo quests. Similarly, gamified platforms can appeal in different ways to different groups.

Game designers have several models of player types that they use as starting points for segmentation. The best known was invented back in the late 1980s by games researcher Richard Bartle, who was studying early text-based multiplayer online games. It wasn't intended as a generalization for all games, let alone all user populations, but it's nonetheless a helpful heuristic for understanding why people play.

Bartle, whom we mentioned in our introduction, distinguished four player types: achievers, explorers, socializers, and killers. Achievers love the rush of leveling up or earning a badge; explorers want to find new content; socializers want to engage with friends; and killers want to impose their will on others, typically by vanquishing them. We all have elements of each of these archetypes. The proportions vary in different settings, and a player's primary motivation can shift over time. The best games and gamified systems have something to offer each category. Even the killers may be your friends if they function as elite "power users" or if they galvanize everyone else in a positive way.

Player modeling is a way to flesh out your segmentation to further guide your design process. Divide your player community into the categories that seem most appropriate. Perhaps you have a group of employees who are focused on proving their mettle to move up in the organization, a group that wants a sense of camaraderie, and a group that wants to feel that the work they do is producing something valuable.

Now, give each group the avatar of a typical player, with a name and a story. An avatar is just a virtual representation of someone. For example, Lucy is a graduate from an Ivy League school who came to work at your firm straight out of college and plans to eventually go back and get her MBA. Bob is a baby boomer, recently retired, who likes to play golf four days a week, and so on. Write a paragraph about each avatar. Where do they fit among the Bartle player types? What are their hopes and fears? Their talents? Their hobbies?

The more detailed the description of the avatars, the better. If the avatars don't ring true, if they don't reflect your likely audience, change them until they do. As you proceed in your gamification process, these character models will ground your design activities. It's easy to imagine how Lucy will respond to a particular quest mechanic. It's less easy to imagine how a nebulous Player A will respond to the same mechanic. And having a small number of representative avatars means that you can understand more easily how your system will appeal to different parts of your audience. It's easy to design for four representative avatars—Lucy, Bob, Layla, and Faraz—but it's hard to design for audience segments like "white, well-educated female players between 25 and 40," "blue-collar male players who don't like games," and so on.

The final dimension to consider is the player lifecycle. Everyone starts as a novice, sometimes called a newbie or "noob" in game circles. Novices need hand-holding to learn the ropes. They may need reinforcement so that they can succeed or so that their friends are also involved. Once the novice becomes a regular, he or she needs novelty in order to stick with the activity. What was at first new and challenging is now effortless. Finally, the player becomes an expert. Experts need challenges that are hard enough to keep them engaged. They also tend to want explicit reinforcement of their status. All your players won't be at the same stage at the same time, although the longer your system runs, the more it will skew toward the experienced end. You must offer opportunities for players at all stages.

4. Devise Your Activity Cycles

Games always have a beginning and sometimes have an end, but along the way they operate through a series of loops and branching trees. In other words, the game isn't simply linear: *Step 1 → Step 2 → Step 3 → Completion.* There may be a leveling system that looks that way, but the overall gamification system behind the scenes isn't so simple. If it were, the system would just be a lockstep series of stages. The most useful way to model the action in a gamified system is through activity cycles, a concept that has gained traction in describing social media and social networking services. User actions provoke some other activity, which in turn provokes other user actions, and so forth. Think of a user tagging a friend in a photo she uploads to Facebook, the upload triggering a notification message to the second user, the second user posting a comment on the photo, a new notification going back to the first user, and so forth.

There are two kinds of cycles to develop: engagement loops and progression stairs. Engagement loops describe, at a micro level, what your players do, why they do it, and what the system does in response. Progression stairs give a macro perspective on the player's journey.

Engagement Loops

Player actions result from motivation and in turn produce feedback in the form of responses from the system, like awarding points. That feedback in turn motivates the user to take further actions, and so on. The key element here is feedback. Feedback is part of what makes games so effective as motivators. Actions immediately produce visible responses. You see immediately where you stand, and when you do something good you always know it.

Virtually all the game components can be seen as forms of feedback. Points, for example, are a way of displaying feedback about performance, as are leaderboards, levels, and achievements. Thinking in terms of feedback keeps you from overemphasizing the specific components or their reward aspects. A reward, after all, is just a kind of feedback. The feedback is what creates the motivation for further actions.

The engagement loop is the basic process of your gamified system. However, it doesn't capture the ways that players advance. Game design consultant Amy Jo Kim points out that gamification experts often come from the world of social media, where quick, temporary relationships are the norm, rather than from the games community, where deep sustained engagement is the goal. They, therefore, have a blind spot in recognizing the importance of the player journey. If the experience is exactly the same on Day 100 as it is on Day 1, most players will get bored. That's where progression stairs come in.

Figure 5.2
Activity Cycle

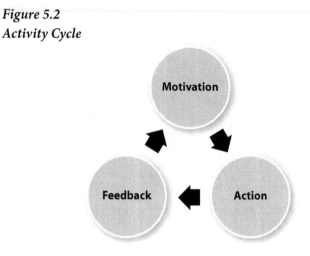

Progression Stairs

Progression stairs reflect the fact that the game experience changes as players move through it. That usually means an escalating level of challenges. In a game such as World of Warcraft, moving from Level 1 to Level 2 takes far less time and experience points than moving from Level 20 to Level 21, and in turn from Level 84 to Level 85. In a gamified system, that equivalent might be the spacing between reward tiers. Map out the player journey in your gamified system as a collection of short-term missions and long-term goals, which play out as a rolling series of progressions.

Though escalating difficulty is the overall tenor of progression, the process shouldn't be completely linear. That's where the progression stair comes in. The very first stair—often called onboarding—needs to be so simple and guided that it draws players into the game. Once the player is over that hurdle, difficulty ideally should increase at variable rates, along what are called interest curves.

The model used in most games involves steadily increasing difficulty, followed by a period of relative ease, followed by a major challenge at the end of each segment. The rest period allows players to catch their breath. It also lets them experience the satisfaction of mastery: the feeling that they've become an expert at some part of the game. There are often a series of small cycles of this sort. The final challenge of a level, known in games as the boss fight, provides for a different experience of mastery. The greatest challenges, which players can just barely surmount, are the ones that produce the explosion of positive emotions that in game terms is called an epic win.

In a gamified system, of course, there probably won't be a "boss" villain waiting at the end of the line. The equivalent is a major challenge that taxes players sufficiently to feel a sense of pride when they reach the next plateau.

Don't neglect to incorporate some measure of randomness. As we noted at Level 4, people like surprises. Studies show that our brains prefer a small, random chance of a big reward to a certainty of a modest reward that over time averages out to a higher number. One only need look at the popularity of slot machines to confirm this finding. Surprises, even small positive surprises, are the way to escape from what is known as the hedonic treadmill: the tendency to take each advance for granted and demand bigger and bigger

Figure 5.3
Progression Stairs

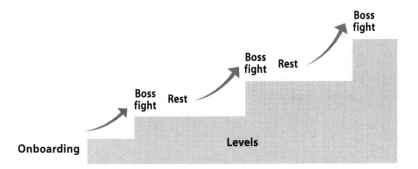

rewards to stave off boredom. Games do this by sometimes giving you a totally unexpected bonus, or by having one treasure chest out of ten, say, stuffed with far more gold than the others.

5. Don't Forget the Fun!

The last thing to do before you start implementing a gamified system is to take a step back and ask a simple question: Is it fun?

In piecing together game elements and attending to the complexities of players, goals, rules, and motivation, it's easy to lose sight of the fun aspect. We see this often with our students in their gamification projects: they get too wrapped up in the details. Gamification done right is serious business, after all. Yet fun should never be far from your mind. If users perceive the gamified system as fun, they are likely to come back. It behooves you to constantly assess the aesthetic appeal of your system and consider whether it's fun to play.

Ask yourself the following question: Would players participate in your system voluntarily? If there weren't any extrinsic rewards offered, would they still be likely to play? If the answer is no, then you should think about what might make your system more fun.

There are many dimensions to fun. Nicole Lazzaro, a game designer and consultant who is an expert on the emotional aspects of games, found four distinct kinds of fun in studying a group of game players. "Hard fun" is a challenge or puzzle, which is fun because of the pleasure of overcoming it. "Easy fun" is casual enjoyment, a way of blowing off steam without overly taxing yourself. The third category, which Lazzaro calls "altered states," we'll call experimental fun. It's the enjoyment of trying out new personas and new experiences. Finally, what Lazzaro calls "the people factor" is essentially social fun: the kinds of fun that depend on interaction with others, even if competitive. Other game designers, notably Marc LeBlanc, offer their own descriptions of the dimensions of fun, involving features like games as make-believe or games as a means of discovering new territory.

What kinds of fun your gamified system should provide will depend on the context. As with player types, don't assume that everyone will want the same type of fun or that participants won't change. The best games offer a broad spectrum of fun. Maybe you're normally attracted to hard-core challenges, but today you just want to blow off steam with your friends. Ideally, a gamified system should be flexible in the same way.

How do you know, though, if a system will actually be fun? For a never-fail answer to that question, you'll need to buy our next book, available for a modest fee . . .

That's a joke. It's intended to make a point: Fun isn't always easy to predict. If it were, game publishers wouldn't spend tens of millions of dollars building games that fail. Fun is an emergent, contingent property that can be fiendishly hard to pin down. The best way to tell if your system is fun is to build it and test it and refine it through a rigorous design process.

6. Deploy the Appropriate Tools for the Job

Finally, we reach the implementation stage. This is where most descriptions of gamification start: picking the appropriate mechanics and components and coding them into your systems. If you've been following us through the levels, you'll see that there is a lot to understand before you start adopting points, badges, and the like. If you've gone through the design steps in this level, you'll be working from a roadmap rather than merely picking elements out of a hat. You'll know your purpose and your users. The engagement loops you created in the previous step should give you the skeleton of your system. The deployment stage is where you need to pull together the overall experience for your players.

This shouldn't be hard to do in practice, although it's hard to describe the process for every case. As you build your system, you'll see features that emerge from the five Ds that you've already analyzed, and the overall design will come clear. At each stage you'll have to make decisions about what to include and exclude. But that's great. The alternative is to try to build something shiny and cool and then find yourself wondering why it never actually worked. So you'll need to test, and iterate, and learn as you go. Find people playing at games like yours, and ask yourself why. Go back to your project and refine it.

To do gamification well, you'll need a team with a variety of skills. This is not to say that a single person can't implement an effective system—in a startup, for example—but they will need expertise in more than one area. You will need:

- People who understand the business goals of the project; the best game designers in the world may produce something useless if they aren't tethered to the desired strategic objectives

- An understanding of your target group of players and the basics of psychology, which were explained at Level 3

- Game designers, or people who can function like them

- Analytics experts able to make sense of the data your gamified systems generates

- Technologists able to implement your vision

Gamification doesn't require technology, any more than games do. However, it lends itself perfectly to online systems. The details of software interfaces and development environments are well beyond the scope of this book, because they change so fast and because there are so many ways to implement a system. In broad brush, though, you're going to need a way to track interactions with game elements and integrate those results with your existing business systems.

Some or all of these functions may be delivered by an outside consulting firm or service provider. There are already companies that have significant experience and that specialize in implementing gamified systems for organizations.

There are two basic options for the technical implementation of gamified systems. You can build custom implementations yourself or use one of the software-as-a-service offerings. A growing number of startups, including Bunchball, Badgeville, BigDoor, Gigya, and iActionable, offer white-label gamification engines to generate and monitor your system. There are also providers such as Keas, Objective Logistics, Salesforce Rypple, and Practically Green, all mentioned earlier, that deliver packaged gamification solutions for particular vertical markets. The build vs. buy decision here is similar to others in web development and social media. If you choose to go with a service provider, look for one that understands the psychological nuances of gamification. The basic functionality isn't that complicated; the value-add from these providers comes from the consulting, customization, and analytics that enable you to optimize your system.

Conclusions (and Beginnings)

If you follow the design process, there is every chance that you will produce an interesting gamification implementation. But there are no guarantees that it will work. Even thoughtful, smart, and experienced developers have to be flexible.

Lift is a startup incubated by Evan Williams and Biz Stone, founders of the popular social media tool Twitter, and led by Tony Stubblebine, who previously founded CrowdVine, a social networking tool for events. Lift allows users to group around personal goals—losing weight, learning a language, raising money for charity. When Stubblebine and his collaborators first designed and coded Lift, they went through the design process and included a range of established gamification techniques such as we saw in the last level. They thought that this approach would be perfect to encourage users to meet their highest potential. Lift is about helping users track progress to any goal, after all; you would think that adding points and badges would be perfect to motivate users toward their goals.

But they quickly discovered that these elements created all manner of problems: They straightjacketed users into a way of thinking that they didn't like, they were unnecessarily complex, they caused tracking and programming problems, and so on. So Lift jettisoned these elements, went back to the drawing board, and came up with different elements—including a simple "props" button to provide encouragement, and feedback loops based on nothing more complicated than a personal history showing how the user did on a weekly or monthly basis. Though Lift is still in its early stages, it's clear that these new design choices suit the overall aims of the business better than their initial reliance on established gamification approaches.

This shouldn't be seen as a failure of gamification or of the design process. Design is an iterative process, and one that is learned by experience. The trick, then, is to go out there and practice. Start building gamified processes and see how they work. Playtest the design to see what might work and then see what actually does work. Build analytics into your system, change a few things, and see what helps move the needle. Interview your players and see what they liked and didn't like. Go back to the drawing board and start again. There's no shortcut for testing and iteration if you really care about producing a successful gamified system.

Epic Fails
And How to Avoid Them

Epic Fail: *Complete and total failure when success should have been reasonably easy to attain.*
—The Urban Dictionary

You've successfully navigated all the basic levels, but there's one more challenge that can't be ignored. This level is about avoiding traps and dangers. Here we'll level up by learning what not to do. We'll talk about:

- *Legal and ethical problems*
- *How to avoid the lure of "pointsification"*
- *The dangers of gamification*

At our 2011 inaugural gamification symposium, For the Win, at Wharton, we invited Ian Bogost to be the first speaker. Bogost is a game designer and theorist at Georgia Tech, author of books such as *Persuasive Games* and *How to Do Things with Videogames* as well as numerous published games. He's also a leading critic of gamification.

Bogost's talk was somewhat provocatively titled "Gamification Is Bullshit." He argued that the practice was "invented by consultants as a means to capture the wild, coveted beast that is videogames and to domesticate it." In other words, gamification is all marketing hype that even the marketers don't believe. Even worse, he claimed, gamification can be employed for purposes that are not in the best interests of players.

Bogost had earlier created a social game called Cow Clicker, where players clicked endlessly on the image of a cow to accumulate virtual cash (called "mooney"), or paid real money in order to accumulate points and upgrade their cow. There was no objective other than to satirize gamification. Bogost thought that people would play once or twice, get the point, and move on. Even he was surprised when Cow Clicker went viral and tens of thousands of people became obsessed with their cow clicking; even people who should "know better." A computer science professor topped the leaderboard at one point with more than 100,000 mooney, the result of many hours of clicks.

This is Kathy Sierra's "high-fructose corn syrup of motivation" at work. Cow Clicker is (by design) gamification at its worst: pointless yet addicting. It's also a warning that serious businesspeople and other practitioners should take to heart.

In this level, we give you a final tier of advice and explain what not to do. Sometimes this will be about how to avoid making ineffective systems, but for the first part of this level we're going to ask whether you can make gamification systems that are too effective. If gamification overemphasizes points and reward systems, as in Cow Clicker, it can replace the richness of games with shallow interactions that are ultimately self-defeating. Also, we'll talk about how to avoid legal and regulatory problems. Then we'll discuss how, if you're not truly acting in the interests of your players, your system can also raise ethical concerns. Finally, what happens when your players turn the tables on you and game your game?

Figure 6.1
Cow Clicker

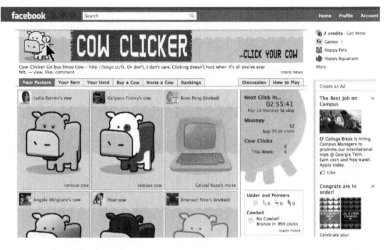

Pointsification

The easiest way to miss the potential of gamification is to focus too heavily on the rewards and not enough on the appeal of the experience. This problem can be seen in the unthinking assumption that any business process can be gamified and improved simply by adding points to it, and motivating users to engage with the system just for the love of collecting points. Hence the name for the criticism: pointsification.

As you learned at Level 4, there's nothing wrong with using points, badges, and leaderboards, or PBLs, in gamification. There's nothing especially right about it, either. Those three elements are the most common components of gamification implementations, to the point where many people think that PBLs are all that gamification is. If the description of your gamified system starts and ends with these three items, chances are you haven't thought it through.

British game developer Margaret Robertson put it well in a much-discussed June 2010 post on her blog, *Hide&Seek*:

What we're currently terming gamification is in fact the process of taking the thing that is least essential to games and representing it as the core of the experience. Points and badges have no closer a relationship to games than they do to websites and fitness apps and loyalty cards. . . . They are the least important bit of a game, the bit that has the least to do with all of the rich cognitive, emotional and social drivers which gamifiers are intending to connect with.

Pointsification creates challenges that may require time and effort, but these aren't inherently interesting. They aren't likely to hold most players' interest for long. A small number of players will enjoy it, just as a small number obsessively clicked on Cow Clicker; but not many will. Adding rewards to the points can make the engagement more enduring, but as long as the rewards themselves are the motivating goal, they will be extrinsic motivators. We showed at Level 3 how limited and even counterproductive that approach can be. You can have extrinsic rewards in your gamified system, but understand what those rewards can and can't do. Always look for ways to replace them with intrinsically enjoyable experiences.

Recall that a high percentage of existing gamification examples are glorified loyalty programs. The loyalty industry is largely ignorant of the potential of fun. Think about your frequent flyer program for a minute. Does it feel game-like at all? Is there any social aspect of the process? Any competitive or cooperative game dynamic? Most loyalty programs are about extrinsic rewards: nothing more, nothing less. They aren't designed to be enjoyable in and of themselves. And the obscurity of the exchange rate for rewards can ultimately be frustrating for users. Hence the massive float of unused loyalty points.

To the extent loyalty programs activate intrinsic motivators, they generally focus on status. United Airlines' 1K flyers and owners of the American Express Black Card get special perks for their exalted loyalty program status, but the real benefit is that exalted status itself. For customers who place high importance on status, that's a big deal.

Status as a motivator is self-limiting, however, because it doesn't work on everybody, and it taps out as a motivator when too many people can reach the high echelons. And at the end of the day, if the actual value delivered isn't sufficient, status will be a cold comfort. High-tier frequent flyer members will no longer get excited about "automatic upgrades" when they realize first class is always sold out.

To take advantage of the full potential of gamification, loyalty programs should be incorporated into more comprehensive designs. Jazzing up rewards with badges and leaderboards isn't enough. Today's consumers have seen so many point systems that they're more likely to be weary than amused when they come across another one. The way to avoid this fate is to create challenges that players find intrinsically motivating. Imagine a loyalty program that allowed you to go on quests: collect miles from flights to three different countries and receive bonus miles or a token of achievement. Imagine one that allowed you to work toward a challenge with family members, friends, or colleagues and which was linked to a social media site that allowed you to coordinate your activities and brag about what you were doing. Or one that placed you on teams to compete against others to amass points for your favorite charity. And so on.

Of course there are good reasons why frequent flyer programs are only about points. They're cheap and easy, and the executives involved may not want to encourage more engagement with their programs. (Although now that we put it that way, it does seem odd that loyalty programs are so flat and uninteresting, doesn't it?) We're not criticizing loyalty programs. We want to show that even something as points-based as a loyalty program doesn't have to fall into the trap of pointsification.

Our observation here reinforces what we've said throughout the book: Don't think of gamification as a cheap marketing trick; think of it as a deep and subtle engagement technique. A substantial percentage of the gamification examples in the wild today are just pointsification. You can do better.

Legal Issues

Another way your gamified system may fail is by running afoul of legal or regulatory limits. You may not have considered this possibility because there is no body of "gamification law" as such in any legal system in the world. Ignoring legal constraints, however, is a serious mistake.

Your gamification project may run into a variety of legal problems. Some are common for social media and other Web 2.0 services, such as the treatment of personally identifiable information about your users. A few, though, are unique to gamification. No project will run into all these issues, because they depend heavily on the nature of the implementation. For example, labor law applies when the subjects of your system are your employees, while data privacy law applies primarily to customers. There is also significant variation in the law depending on where you're implementing the system. Intellectual property protection is generally tighter in the United States, for example, while labor and advertising rules are stricter in Europe.

If you think your gamified service might raise legal concerns, talk to a lawyer. We're not just saying that because both of the authors have law degrees. Legal experts can advise you on the specific considerations for your particular situation. If they do their job properly, they'll help you understand how much risk you're undertaking and how you could mitigate that risk.

As a practical matter, the way you'll deal with most of these concerns is through your terms of service. The terms of service agreement is the digital contract between the operator and users of an online service. You've agreed to dozens of them, whether you realize it or not. Virtually every time you register for a web-based service or e-commerce site, there will be a link next to the confirmation button for the terms of service. Behind that link is usually an exten-sive contract detailing the legal obligations that customers undertake.

As a general rule, such "clickwrap" agreements are legally binding. Users only need to receive notification that they are agreeing to a contract and a reasonable opportunity to access the full text, even if they don't actually read it. There are some things the courts won't allow you to put into a clickwrap terms of service agreement, but you have a great deal of leeway to anticipate potential legal complications.

Privacy

Privacy is one of the most controversial and uncertain areas of the law for online services. In many countries outside the United States, there are strong data privacy requirements on the books. Businesses often must receive affirmative opt-in consent before collecting any personally identifiable information from users, in addition to other restrictions, such as providing the opportunity for users to review and edit information. The United States tends to be more lenient than other countries, but that may be changing.

Your gamified system can collect a great deal of information about players. As we've discussed, every activity can be tracked. That information can be cross-referenced with other data you have, such as the user's prior transaction history, age, and address. Or you might use gamification to incentivize users to fill out a survey that provides more detailed information about themselves. Make sure you can articulate exactly what personally identifiable information you collect from users, why you collect it, and what you do with it. If you're operating in or sending data to a jurisdiction such as Europe or Canada with more restrictive data privacy rules, you'll need to ensure that your practices comply. This is also true in the United States if you're dealing with sensitive categories of information, such as medical or financial data, or data collected about children.

Aside from understanding specific laws regulating the collection and use of personally identifying information, any designer of a gamified service should produce a privacy policy for it. Your privacy policy functions similarly to your terms of service agreement. It's your representation to your users about what data you will collect, what you'll do with it, and related practices. You're legally obligated to adhere to your privacy policy, but under US law, the policy can be quite permissive. You should keep in mind, however, that public opinion may be more restrictive. Your goal is for your users to enjoy your service, after all, not to anger them. Sometimes the court of public opinion is the strongest court of all.

Finally, good data protection practices also include data security. The last thing you want is for personal data to leak or be stolen, outraging your users.

Intellectual Property

Intellectual property is the body of law granting exclusive legal rights for intellectual assets. Your gamified system may well involve all four major forms of intellectual property: copyright, trademarks, patents, and trade secrets. You'll want to make sure you're taking sufficient steps to protect any unique assets you're creating. Sometimes this will involve expense, such as filing a patent application for your gamified invention. In the case of copyright and trade secrets, and to a lesser extent trademark, protection will usually happen automatically through your commercial activity and normal business practices.

From a defensive standpoint, take care not to infringe on the intellectual property of others. In most cases that will be easy to avoid. For example, if you like the badge designs on another gamified site, you can't simply copy them and use them yourself, unless the creator authorizes it. The area that is likely to involve the greatest legal risk here is from patents. In the United States, both software and business methods are patentable. There have been a number of cases in which holders of questionable patents were able to recoup substantial damages from companies that independently developed similar ideas. Gamification is too new to be the subject of significant patent battles, but it's only a matter of time. We would be very surprised if there haven't been many patent applications already filed over gamification inventions; and the future will see many fights over their validity and use.

Property Rights in Virtual Assets

If the assets in your gamified system are valuable in some way, who owns them? You? Or the players who accumulate them? This question is separate from the intellectual property considerations about your creative activities. If users owned their points or achievement titles, they would have rights. They might be able to resell them or prohibit you from, for example, deciding that henceforth it will take 10,000 points instead of 5,000 to reach the "guru" level.

This issue emerged with virtual worlds such as Second Life, which allowed their users to create virtual assets like buildings and clothing. Generally, courts have found that such assets are merely contractual licenses from the game developers, which do not confer property rights on the users. Be sure your terms of service are clear on this point.

Sweepstakes and Gambling

There are laws in many jurisdictions regulating sweepstakes, gambling, and related activities. These come into play when you are offering prizes of some appreciable monetary value. Depending on the circumstances, your gamified service might be considered a sweepstakes, a lottery, gambling, or a contest. All are significantly regulated but in different ways. If the rewards you're offering are of no actual value, such as a badge or an achievement within the game itself, these rules don't come into play. Similarly, if you're offering your own service as a reward, such as a free cup of coffee to the "mayor" of a Starbucks on Foursquare, the sweepstakes rules usually don't apply.

Deceptive Practices

If your business model is based on fooling users, you're going to run into the various legal rules prohibiting business fraud. This is as true if you're giving out virtual badges as if you're selling stock. The question of deceptive practices can be more complicated for gamification, though, because of the psychological aspects of motivation. What if players are engaged in something because it's fun, but your company financially benefits from their actions?

The basic rule is that users should not be deceived. If they are aware that Procter & Gamble is providing the gamified system as a promotion for one of its products, there's nothing wrong with the fact that they are voluntarily providing marketing benefits for the company. Furthermore, users should not be made to do something against their interest. For example, a gamified system that led users to choose higher credit card interest rates solely to receive nonfinancial virtual rewards would be problematic.

Advertising

If the gamified system functions as advertising, there are rules about what actions are going to cause problems. These include a baseline prohibition on deception, similar to the previous topic. Beyond that, though, the specifics vary a great deal among jurisdictions. As with privacy law, the United States is significantly more lenient than the rest of the world.

Labor

Generally, businesses have more leeway dealing with employees than with consumers, but employers still cannot deliberately deceive employees or force them to act against their own interests. At the extreme, a gamified system that was so addictive it created a compulsion among employees might raise concerns about involuntary servitude, although this would probably be more of an ethical concern than a legal one.

An employee can be required to play a game as part of his or her job, just like any other mandatory job responsibilities. And the employer can generally use performance in a game-like system as a criterion for promotion or firing. This may not be the case in work environments subject to collective bargaining agreements, or in countries such as Germany where work rules must be defined through structured labor-management processes.

Paid Endorsements

In the United States, the Federal Trade Commission has adopted guidelines requiring disclosure of paid endorsements through social media. The rules were designed to deal with personal blogs that hid the fact their views about products were sponsored by the creators of those products. However, these guidelines are broad enough to cover gamification. For example, if your service gives users points or other rewards for recommending your product to their friends on Twitter or Facebook, you might need to consider some disclosure.

Virtual Currency Regulation

Virtual currencies add a significant new dimension of legal risk because they connect to real money. Real currencies are heavily regulated throughout the world to prevent fraud, money laundering, currency manipulation, theft, and other problems. Certain activities involving currencies can only be undertaken by banks, which are subject to a plethora of regulations and restrictions. Accounting and taxation also come into play. This is not to say that it's impossible to offer a virtual currency. Virtual worlds such as Second Life and online games such as Eve Online have done so successfully, but only with careful attention to the legal considerations. Foursquare has also engaged in partnerships with companies such as American Express.

Future Legal Issues

As gamification becomes more common, we expect to see regulators and legislators become more involved. Inevitably, some company will use gamification in a careless or malevolent way, giving rise to a scandal that provokes calls for legal responses. Equally inevitably, some of the proposed responses will be overreactions crafted by people who don't understand gamification. The best you can do is to keep your eyes open for such developments. And most important, make sure the subject of the scandal isn't you.

The final point to make about legal rules is that you should view them as a floor rather than as a ceiling. This is a fast-changing area, so a borderline practice that seems legally permissible today may be prohibited tomorrow. Moreover, compliance with the law isn't always enough to keep you out of trouble. Ethical and reputational considerations extend above and beyond what law may require. We turn to them next.

Exploitationware

Laundry workers at Disneyland hotels in Anaheim, California, have a name for the leaderboard system the company installed in 2011: "the electronic whip." Large flat-panel monitors in laundry rooms show employees how quickly they fulfill their tasks and how their speed compares to co-workers'. The system has certainly had an effect. Relationships between workers are increasingly tense as the work environment becomes more competitive. Some are even skipping bathroom breaks to bump up their numbers. Those low in the rankings worry about their job security.

Perhaps this is what Disney intended. Constant quantitative performance monitoring isn't new, for these hotel laundry workers or for many employees in structured, routine jobs. Public leaderboards are just a logical next step. The Disney system isn't a full-blown gamification implementation, since it only uses the rankings inherent in a leaderboard. But badges, avatars, and achievements can't be far behind, can they? Whether the efficiency gains of the electronic whip exceed the costs in worker dissatisfaction is a question only Disney can answer. In evaluating your gamification initiatives, it needs to be a consideration.

The Disney example isn't atypical. Research has shown that leaderboards alone in the workplace are generally demotivating, especially for women. In some contexts, such as sales, contests may be so pervasive that the effects are less significant, but they still show up. The problem isn't leaderboards per se. The real issue is any motivational techniques that operate through fear rather than fun. Any athlete who's had butterflies before a big game knows that games can bring out unpleasant emotions along with the positive ones.

At one level, this discussion is a microcosm of normal HR considerations. There has been plenty of analysis on the best ways to motivate employees, and there are many different models that one could point to. However, because gamification is a form of motivational design, it puts a finer point on considerations of employee empowerment and enjoyment. You can use gamification, as Disney did, to control employees more tightly and push them more aggressively. But that forgoes all the benefits of intrinsic motivation. In the end it's important to remember that gamification works over the long run by making things more enjoyable rather than more stressful.

Back at Level 2, we explained that games are defined, in part, by voluntariness. If your employer orders you to play ping-pong and declares that your salary will be directly proportional to your score, you're not really playing a game. You may go through the same motions as your opponent, who plays by choice, but your experience is very different. If employers force gamification on their workers, it can undermine the motivational benefits of the activity. When the system is designed well, compulsion shouldn't be necessary. LiveOps, the call-center outsourcer we profiled in Level 3, makes its gamified tools voluntary for its agents. Eighty percent of them choose to use them, and of those, 95% remain active.

For external (consumer-facing) gamification, users can always stop playing. There's no threat of cutting salary or firing held over their head. However, gamification done well creates powerful motivational impulses. If participants feel they can't stop, is gamification effectively a form of compulsion? Should it be treated like gambling or smoking, which are regulated because of their addictive potential? Ian Bogost argues that gamification should instead be called "exploitationware," because it exploits people to do things against their interests or beliefs.

We wouldn't go that far, but Bogost raises a legitimate concern. We don't know how gamification is going to be used in the future, and it may be employed for evil rather than for good. But in general we think the worry is overblown. At the beginning of modern advertising practice we saw a range of critiques about how advertising, especially television advertising, was taking away people's free will and turning them into zombies. This moral panic culminated in widespread antipathy toward subliminal advertising, which was supposed to be able to convince you to do things—buy cigarettes, drink Coke—through images and messages that you weren't even aware of. The efficacy of subliminal advertising is now discredited, but the concern and anger over it lingers to this day.

Concerns about the antilibertarian possibilities of gamification are similar to concerns over subliminal advertising. It's true that games can be compelling. Every now and again there are calls for restricting the number of hours that kids can play massively multiplayer online games, and apocryphal stories of Asian kids who played so long that they collapsed and died from exhaustion. Not only are these stories overblown, they're never going to be an issue for gamification. It turns out that individual game mechanics such as we find in gamification are not so addictive that they need to be regulated. The problem with gamification is almost always that it's not fun enough; not that it's too much fun.

If they're not dangerous, then why do people still feel uncomfortable when they hear about game elements being used in marketing or enterprise or social impact settings? In part, there is discomfort over the fact that something people enjoy could be used to profit others. We think that everyone should be able to exercise free will and choose what he or she wants to do. Another consideration is the shock of the new: We are uncertain how we should feel about these sorts of things because we've never seen them before.

As the world becomes more familiar with gamification, we'll see that the dystopian nightmares are found only in our imaginations. However, there are some scenarios where special caution should be taken. For example, it is possible to use gamification to mask objectionable activities. Imagine that you created a game wherein people matched security photos with mugshots, which turned out to be a way of tracking people without their consent. Deceiving people about your purposes, even if they find the game fun, is both an ethical breach and likely to cause ongoing problems. Eventually people will find out, and the public relations blowback will be severe. Outside such special cases, we think that gamification will come to be seen as one of many methods of regulating people's behavior and will be subject to the natural limit that we always find with these sorts of regulators. In the end, people will be themselves. And there's only so much that you can do to influence that.

This leads to our final cautionary note. Because sometimes users act in ways you don't expect.

Gaming the Game

A system that incorporates intrinsic motivation will produce a sense of autonomy or agency. Your players need to feel that, in some meaningful way, they are in control. By far the best way to inculcate this feeling is to give them control. That, however, creates its own challenges.

Game designer and consultant Nicole Lazzaro of XEODesign gives the example of the toll system for the Bay Bridge in San Francisco. To encourage drivers to avoid rush hour, the toll goes down significantly at night. The problem with this incentive system is that it encourages some users to play it as a game. Some cars approaching the bridge close to the cut-off time for the lower toll pull off to the shoulder in order to wait. When enough cars do so suddenly, it creates a dangerous traffic situation that the designers of the dynamic pricing system didn't anticipate.

Users may find it more enjoyable to play a game of their own choosing than the one you've laid out for them. Often this takes the form of exploration. Among the most popular pursuits in "open world" videogames such as Grand Theft Auto is to go off the roads (literally) and see what you can find. But in any gamified system you should expect users to test the edges of your system to see what is there.

The other thing players are likely to do is game the system. If the goals in the gamified system are interesting to the players, some of them will look for ways to cut corners. There are often many ways to do so that don't necessarily amount to cheating. The more the gamified system gives players options, the more likely they will find opportunities that the designers never anticipated.

Lloyds TSB Bank implemented an internal market for innovation ideas. It gave its employees a virtual currency, called Beanz, and asked them to submit and rate ideas. The highest-ranked ideas were placed into a virtual stock market, allowing employees to "buy" and "sell" using their Beanz. The Beanz could be cashed out for real money.

The Lloyds system worked exactly as designed . . . except that users acted in unanticipated ways. First, the virtual economy took off, to the point where there was hyperinflation that was so serious that the supply of Beanz was restricted. Then players realized there was a way to improve their performance on the virtual stock market: insider trading. By affiliating with groups developing ideas, they were able to obtain better information than ordinary "investors" and cash in.

James Gardner, who created the system for Lloyds and went on to develop similar gamified innovation markets at other organizations, says that initially his instinct was to stamp out the insider trading. But he quickly realized that this emergent behavior was a feature rather than a bug. The goal of the whole process, after all, was to encourage Lloyds employees to work together more efficiently and develop creative ideas for innovation. In gaming the idea market, employees were doing just that. Working together with the top innovators was the best way to win the game but also the best way to achieve the company's ultimate goals for the project. (If the aim of the project was to stamp out insider trading, presumably the company would have had a different view of the unintended behavior.)

As the Lloyds example demonstrates, users gaming the system can be both beneficial and detrimental. Hyperinflation of virtual currency threatened to destroy the virtual marketplace, but insider trading actually enhanced it. The sense of autonomy that users experienced when finding unplanned ways to exploit a gamified system also reinforced their intrinsic engagement. You need to be careful in some settings, such as if you are exchanging virtual currency for valuable goods, since this can encourage criminal behavior. But otherwise gaming the system is something to anticipate and encourage, not discourage.

Always remember that your players are people, too. They won't always act in the ways you expect them to. If gamification were just a simple algorithm where input A generated output B, it wouldn't produce particularly interesting results. The whole reason to incorporate elements of play into business situations is because fun has a powerful pull that logic can't match. For all the analytics and technical manifestations, that makes gamification fundamentally human. The most successful practitioners recognize that people like them, with all their talents and foibles, are on the other side of the screen.

Endgame
In Conclusion

> *I think work is the world's greatest fun.*
> —Thomas Edison

You've made it to the final level. Here we look back on what we've covered and forward to the future of gamification.

Consider the experience of Rochester Institute of Technology's School of Interactive Games and Media, one of America's top-ranked game-design programs. In 2011 Professors Elizabeth Lawley, Andy Phelps, and Elouise Oyzon resolved to gamify their entire student experience. The project—called Just Press Play—aims to overhaul how we motivate students in higher education. (We're both on the advisory board.)

Rather than redesigning their courses, the project team took a hard look at the things that students really need and what improves their learning outcomes. They discovered that students perform better when they know at least one professor to call on for advice; they are happier when they know their way around campus and around town; they do better when they know how to work in teams; and they do much better when they are connected with the community of learning within the entire school. Most of these things you can't build into a curriculum; but you can do it with a game.

To encourage them to get to know their professors, the Just Press Play team printed up collectible cards that students receive in person from a professor when they undertake a quest that the professor designates. One professor, David Simkins, has hidden his collectible cards in his office, and students have to engage him in conversation as they hunt around his books trying to find their prize. They don't even notice that they're getting to know the professor. They just want the card.

Just Press Play also has achievements that students must perform as a team, not just as individuals, so that they learn how to work together. For years the faculty struggled to raise the pass rate on the freshman programming exam. Nothing they did seemed to make a difference. Just Press Play included a collective achievement that every first-year student would receive . . . but only if over 90% of them passed the exam.

The designers hoped this would motivate students to work hard, and perhaps a few of the more talented first years might give a hand to the less capable ones. What they didn't anticipate was a number of the juniors and seniors showing up in the computer lab, asking freshmen if they needed help. There was no achievement available to the upper-level students. They were doing it not for a reward but because they thought the whole game was deeply cool, and they wanted to be a part of it.

Lo and behold, the pass rate on the exam was the highest ever. The freshmen got their badges. The real rewards went far beyond that. In fact, the juniors and seniors enjoyed the peer-to-peer study sessions so much that they asked for permission to run similar groups every quarter.

Just Press Play shows how you can use a game-like system to motivate behavior that is important but usually ignored. It is hard to teach teamwork within a normal undergraduate class, so we usually don't bother to try. And no class that we're aware of ever assesses a student on whether he or she can find the office of a professor. But these things turn out to be vitally important to learning, and they can be built into a gamified environment. The flexibility of gamification allowed the RIT professors to identify what they wanted their freshmen to do—"Define your Business Objective" in our six Ds from Level 5—even though it wasn't within the standard curriculum. And then they worked through the other levels that we've discussed and built a gamified system around that objective.

Not all gamification efforts are as compelling. Sometimes a project swings for the fences but, for whatever reason, misses the ball. An example is the Attent system from Seriosity, one of the earliest thoughtful efforts to engage in internal gamification. Attent uses a form of virtual currency, called "serios," to encourage people to use email more effectively. Serios are used within subscribing enterprises to send and read email, and heavy users of email can buy and sell serios like any virtual currency. The idea seems like a sound one, since the resource constraints in virtual currencies are fun and powerful behavior regulators.

Seriosity is a pioneering company led by brilliant Stanford researchers and experienced entrepreneurs. Yet its attempt to gamify email never really caught on with users. Implementing the virtual economy in Attent was problematic. At one point, a member of Seriosity's advisory board said that he would only read his outside emails if serios came attached to messages. When numerous friends and colleagues said that they would never buy serios just to email him, he was forced to retract the statement.

The point here is not to single out Seriosity. Even successful gamification adopters experience bumps in the road or false turns. Seriosity was ahead of its time and may yet strike gold in applying game mechanics to email. More recently, a startup called Baydin launched The Email Game, which rewards users with levels and points based on the speed with which they process their email. It claims good results, but the jury is still out when it comes to widespread adoption. These examples demonstrate that we're still at the birth of serious gamification. For every successful implementation like RIT's Just Press Play, we'll see five or ten attempts that will fall flat or have limited impact. That's exactly what happened with social media (there were many Jaikus for every Twitter); and it's what happened with e-commerce (there were multiple Webvans for every Amazon.com).

This book has been about trying to extract as many lessons as possible from the gamification state of art, so that your efforts will be counted among the successful few. In this final level it's worthwhile looking back at the lessons we've learned and casting our gaze forward to see what the future of gamification may look like.

Looking Back

What have we learned?

First, while points, badges, and leaderboards may be important elements of some projects, gamification is more than just drizzling these element onto a business process like caramel syrup on a sundae. Gamification requires a great deal of thought about the entire design of the system, including understanding the nature of your users, thinking about what you'd like them to do and how best to make them do it, considering the best technology platform to do that, and examining the specific game elements you're going to employ to get them to do things—among many other considerations.

Along the way we've also learned some very specific lessons about how to implement gamification design. We've developed lessons in motivation and behavior modification that work. We've sketched out ways of thinking about your users. We've discussed methods of connecting different game elements, and when you should and should not use them. And we've seen numerous examples of successful and unsuccessful gamification in a range of disciplines— including your own, one hopes.

One of the most important lessons, however, has gone largely unstated. Our view is that businesspeople need to learn from games, but at the same time, game designers need to learn from business experts. Juho Hamari and Vili Lehdonvirta, two Finnish researchers, studied the way popular massively multiplayer online games from around the world handled virtual goods. They found that their practice mirrored established marketing concepts, including segmentation, product differentiation, lifecycle management, and exploitation of cognitive biases. What's interesting is that the game designers weren't getting these ideas by talking to marketers in non-game industries. They were reinventing them in response to the behavior of their players. The same story is playing out in the gamification world.

This is where you, the readers of this book, come in. The most successful new gamification efforts will come from people schooled in "traditional" areas of business, philanthropy, and government who take the lessons from this book and apply them to fields that they understand and know. Gamification may be the next new thing, but its future will depend on linkages to established fields.

Looking Forward

What, then, of the future?

To some extent, we can expect more of the same, only bigger. We'll be amazed if in a couple of years' time any executive can get away with a sales and marketing plan that doesn't consider gamification in some form, just like online and social media today. We'll see more innovative examples like the one that gamification startup SCVNGR produced for Buffalo Wild Wings during the March Madness college basketball tournament. Users won free stuff at the restaurant chain by completing challenges like stacking multiple burgers on end or taking photos with a fan of an opposing team. We'll see challengers to Foursquare and other providers in retail marketing, who provide turnkey gamification solutions and access to huge audiences through social media. Companies like Facebook and Zynga will buy gamification providers and systems and will tie gamification more explicitly to social media platforms.

We think that it's likely we'll start to see internal gamification in many more business arenas, and that it will become more important in enterprise situations. Imaginative executives will build it out into fields that we haven't seen before and use it to increase productivity in most parts of business. We'll probably see this happen first in human resources and sales, where motivating staff is already a well-known process and is ripe for overhaul. But we'll also see it in areas that we haven't witnessed before: Just as Ross Smith transformed language localization of dialog boxes at Microsoft, some enterprising executives will find a way to transform parts of accounting, strategy, product design, and the like.

We think gamification will have a huge impact in government and politics, as well as in charitable, philanthropic, and social impact arenas. These arenas are ripe for gamification because these activities are not primarily about money. They have typically used mechanisms like altruism or guilt to motivate supporters. It's clear than fun can fit into this framework quite neatly and supplement those motivators. We've already discussed some examples of behavior-change gamification in social impact settings, and we'll see many more in the near future. The 2012 American Presidential campaign represents the first time that gamification was used extensively in the political process. It won't be the last.

Beyond these basic observations, we can't predict the future of gamification. We are convinced it will become more mainstream in the coming years. In time the hype will die, replaced by the recognition that gamification can deliver results. As long as the design is thought through properly, gamification will work and will just be seen as part of the modern executive's toolkit.

Eventually gamification will be important to every part of business, even if it doesn't transform all of them.

If nothing else, it may make business more fun.

Acknowledgments

This book would not have been possible without the support and assistance of many people.

Kevin would like to thank Justin Dunham, Roz Duffy, Karl Ulrich, Ethan Mollick, and Adam Werbach for their contributions to the project. And to Johanna, thanks for being there.

Dan would like to thank Naomi Allen, Stephanie Chichetti, Jill Raines, and Jennifer Williams for their excellent assistance and feedback.

We both express our sincere gratitude to Philip Beauregard, Adam Bosworth, Sebastian Deterding, Caryn Effron, David Johnson, Amy Jo Kim, Liz Lawley, Greg Lastowka, Nicole Lazzaro, Thomas Malaby, Andy Phelps, J. P. Rangaswami, Jesse Redniss, Ross Smith, Kurt Squire, Susan Hunt Stevens, and Tony Stubblebine for thoughtful comments on the manuscript or insights in conversation. Steve Kobrin and Shannon Berning of Wharton Digital Press provided excellent editorial support and an opportunity to explore an innovative new form of publishing. The members of the Terror Nova World of Warcraft guild showed us just how much fun games can be. The participants in the 2011 For the Win symposium proved that even the experts are still making sense of this emerging field. And the students in our inaugural gamification course at Wharton were the best teachers we could possibly have.

Glossary

Advergames. Games built to promote products or services. Commonly used to increase activity or brand engagement on consumer-facing websites.

Avatar. A virtual representation of a player's character in a game. Common in role-playing games in which the player might take on the role of a magical creature or a medieval warrior.

Badge. A visual token of an achievement. Usually designed to look like the real-world analogs, such as Boy Scout badges or the Good Housekeeping Seal.

Boss fight. A difficult fight against a high-level opponent, called a boss. Often marks the end of a level or a section of a game.

Daily/monthly active users (DAUs/MAUs). The number of individuals who visit your website on an average day or during the course of a month. Common metrics for social games. The ratio of these numbers indicates the intensity of user activity; a DAU/MAU ratio of 50% would mean that half the users visit every day.

Engagement loop. The basic cycle of activity in a game, from motivation to activity to feedback, which in turn motivates further actions.

Epic fail. A major screw-up in a game, such as dying quickly in combat or falling off a ledge by accident.

Epic win. A glorious victory in a game, usually stretching players to the limits of their abilities. Often connected to a boss fight or finishing a game.

Extrinsic motivation. Doing something for a reason other than for its own sake. This could be money, status, power, some other reward you value, direction by your boss, benefits for someone else you care about, and so on.

Foursquare. A mobile social location application for smartphones, which encourages users to check in at their current location to find information about the venue and other users who have done so.

Game. A voluntary activity that operates within a "magic circle," in which players follow the rules of the game rather than those of the real world.

Game component. A particular structure in a game, implementing the game's mechanics and dynamics. Points and badges are examples of game components.

Game design. The overall process of creating engaging games, based on an understanding of player desires, technological feasibility, and business objectives. Distinguished from the narrower term "game development," which is the technical implementation of a game.

Game dynamic. The conceptual structures underlying a game, such as the narrative and rules (constraints) that shape the game. These are the most abstract game elements. Players feel their effects but do not engage with them directly.

Game element. A design pattern that can be incorporated into a game. Game elements are the pieces that a game designer assembles in creating an engaging experience.

Game mechanics. The processes that drive forward the action in a game, such as feedback or turns. Game mechanics are the actions that implement higher-level game dynamics and manifest themselves in lower-level game components.

Game thinking. The process of addressing problems like a game designer, by looking at how to motivate players and create engaging, fun experiences. Sometimes called "gameful thinking," in contrast to unstructured "playful thinking."

Games for change. Serious games created for some social benefit, ranging from improving health and wellness to educating kids about the US political process.

Gamification. The use of game elements and game thinking in non-game contexts.

Interest curve. The pattern of gradually increasing difficulty in a game, structured to keep users interested at every stage. Typically, initial levels are easy and quick, to get players hooked, while end-game levels are difficult and long to provide sufficient challenges for experienced players.

Intrinsic motivation. Doing something for its own sake. People are intrinsically motivated if they engage in activity without any hope of an external reward. According to Self-Determination Theory, such activities evoke feelings of competence, autonomy, and relatedness.

Leaderboard. A ranked list of participants in a game, with the highest scores on top.

Loyalty program. A program to reward regular customers with benefits in proportion to their level of activity. Airline frequent flyer programs are the classic example.

Magic circle. The virtual or physical space where the rules of the game hold sway over those of the real world. The concept was introduced by early twentieth-century Dutch philosopher Johan Huizinga.

Massively multiplayer online game (MMOG). Games such as World of Warcraft, in which thousands or even millions of players interact in the same online virtual world. Many such games involve role-playing in fantasy or science fiction settings and are sometimes called massively multiplayer online role-playing games (MMORPGs).

Operant conditioning. A theory and process developed by psychologist B. F. Skinner in which behavior is modified by rewards (and, in some approaches, by punishment also).

Play. An essentially unconstrained experience of spontaneous fun, contrasted with the structured rule-based systems of games.

Playtesting. Trying out a game with actual players as a way of garnering feedback. Playtesting can occur with rough versions of a game or even through the use of paper descriptions of gameplay.

Progression stairs. The cycle of advancement through the levels or other steps in a game. Essentially, a more detailed version of the game's interest curve, in which challenges are often followed by rest or consolidation periods along a generally upward trajectory.

Quest. A specific mission or challenge for players of a game. The quest will usually have a narrative and an objective ("collect six Delicious Toadstools from the cave guarded by the Old Troll") and a reward for completion.

Self-Determination Theory. A psychological theory developed by Edward Deci and Richard Ryan of the University of Rochester, along with many collaborators, which defines and emphasizes the importance of intrinsic motivation.

Serious games. Games created for a purpose other than enjoyment, typically some form of knowledge or skill development.

Social games. Online games delivered through social networks, primarily Facebook, often with a significant element of social interaction. The most successful social games developer is Zynga, publisher of FarmVille, Words With Friends, Mafia Wars, and Draw Something.

Social graph. The network of relationships among friends, such as the matrix of connections on Facebook or other social networking sites.

Variable reward schedule. A prize or reward delivered on some nonpredictable basis, such as the payoff of a slot machine. Contrasted with fixed interval rewards (guaranteed at regular time periods) or fixed-ratio rewards (guaranteed for a certain amount of activity).

Virtual currency. A medium of exchange in a game, allowing players to purchase virtual goods or other benefits.

Virtual economy. A functional market system in a game, typically including virtual currency and virtual goods that are subject at least in part to economic forces.

Virtual goods. Virtual items that have value or uniqueness within a game environment. Players may be able to purchase virtual goods with virtual currency, real money, or through achievements within the game. Also called virtual assets.

Virtual world. A persistent online community that allows for virtual interactions between players. Typically virtual worlds involve immersive 3D environments, although this is not essential. Most are online role-playing games, but some virtual worlds, such as Second Life, have no gameplay objectives.

Win state. The outcomes of a game that constitute "winning." Typically defined by the rules of the game and the game's feedback or rewards mechanisms.

World of Warcraft. The most successful massively multiplayer online game, a fantasy role-playing world introduced in 2005 by Activision Blizzard. Also known as WoW, it peaked at 12 million paying users worldwide.

Additional Resources

If you are looking to go beyond this book, our website, www.gamifyforthewin.com, has additional information on gamification and related concepts.

Here are some references that you may find valuable. These works are generally not about gamification per se; they expand on relevant concepts that we introduce in this book.

Bogost, Ian. *Persuasive Games: The Expressive Power of Videogames.* Cambridge, MA: MIT Press, 2007.

Castronova, Edward. *Synthetic Worlds: The Business and Culture of Online Games.* Chicago, IL: University of Chicago Press, 2005.

Deterding, Sebastian, Dan Dixon, Rilla Khaled, and Lennart Nacke. "From Game Design Elements to Gamefulness: Defining Gamification," Proceedings of the 15th International Academic MindTrek Conference: Envisioning Future Media Environments. City New York, NY: ACM Press, 2011.

Edery, David, and Ethan Mollick. *Changing the Game: How Video Games Are Transforming the Future of Business.* Upper Saddle River, NJ: FT Press, 2009.

Gee, James Paul. *What Video Games Have to Teach Us About Learning and Literacy.* New York, NY: Palgrave Macmillan, 2003.

Koster, Raph. *A Theory of Fun for Game Design.* Scottsdale, AZ: Paraglyph Press, 2005.

Lazzaro, Nicole. "Why We Play Games: Four Keys to More Emotion Without Story." 2004. http://www.xeodesign.com/xeodesign_whyweplaygames.pdf.

McGonigal, Jane. *Reality Is Broken: Why Games Make Us Better and How They Can Change the World.* New York, NY: Penguin, 2011.

Pink, Daniel. *Drive: The Surprising Truth About What Motivates Us.* New York, NY: Riverhead, 2009.

Radoff, Jon. *Game On: Energize Your Business with Social Media Games.* Indianapolis, IN: Wiley, 2011.

Reeves, Byron, and J. Leighton Read. *Total Engagement: Using Games and Virtual Worlds to Change the Way People Work and Businesses Compete.* Boston, MA: Harvard Business School Publishing, 2009.

Rigby, Scott, and Richard Ryan. *Glued to Games: How Video Games Draw Us In and Hold Us Spellbound.* Santa Barbara, CA: Praeger, 2011.

Robertson, Margaret, "Can't Play, Won't Play," *Hide&Seek*, http://www.hideandseek.net/2010/10/06/cant-play-wont-play/, October 6, 2010.

Salen, Katie, and Eric Zimmerman. *Rules of Play: Game Design Fundamentals.* Cambridge, MA: MIT Press, 2004.

Schell, Jesse. *The Art of Game Design: A Book of Lenses.* Burlington, MA: Morgan Kaufmann, 2008.

Sheldon, Lee. *The Multiplayer Classroom: Designing Coursework as a Game.* Boston, MA: Cengage Learning, 2012.

Squire, Kurt. *Video Games and Learning: Teaching and Participatory Culture in the Digital Age.* New York: Teachers College Press, 2011.

Thomas, Douglas, and John Seely Brown. *A New Culture of Learning: Cultivating the Imagination for a World of Constant Change.* CreateSpace, 2011.

Index

About the Authors

Kevin Werbach is a leading expert on the legal, business, and public policy aspects of the Network Age. He is an associate professor of Legal Studies at The Wharton School, University of Pennsylvania, and the founder of Supernova Group, a technology consulting firm. He co-led the review of the Federal Communications Commission for the Obama Administration's Presidential Transition Team and served as an expert adviser on broadband issues to the FCC and the National Telecommunications and Information Administration. For nine years he organized Supernova, a leading executive technology conference. Werbach was previously the editor of "Release 1.0: Esther Dyson's Monthly Report," and served as Counsel for New Technology Policy at the FCC in the Clinton administration, where he helped develop the U.S. government's Internet and e-commerce policies. He has written numerous scholarly and popular articles on a wide range of technology topics and appears frequently as an expert in print, online, and broadcast media. A graduate of UC–Berkeley and Harvard Law School, he is a fellow of the Global Institute for Communications, a director of Public Knowledge, an advisory council member for the Institute for the Future, and an editorial board member of Wharton Digital Press, *Info, I/S,* and the *Journal of Information Policy*. He blogs at http://werblog.com and tweets at @kwerb.

Dan Hunter is an expert in Internet law, intellectual property, and the application of games to public policy arenas. He is a professor of law at New York Law School and the director of the school's Institute for Information Law & Policy. He is also an adjunct associate professor of legal studies at The Wharton School, University of Pennsylvania. He previously taught law at the University of Melbourne, was a tenured professor at The Wharton School, University of Pennsylvania, and taught on the law faculty at Cambridge University. He regularly publishes on issues dealing with the intersection of computers and law, including papers dealing with the regulation of virtual worlds and video games, as well as high-technology aspects of intellectual property. He was one of the first scholars to examine the social significance of massively multiplayer online games, and cofounded the scholarly blog *Terra Nova* (terranova.blogs.com). This is his fourth book.

About Wharton Digital Press

Wharton Digital Press was established to inspire bold, insightful thinking within the global business community. In the tradition of The Wharton School of the University of Pennsylvania and its online business journal, *Knowledge@Wharton*, Wharton Digital Press uses innovative digital technologies to help managers meet the challenges of today and tomorrow.

As an entrepreneurial publisher, Wharton Digital Press delivers relevant, accessible, conceptually sound, and empirically based business knowledge to readers wherever and whenever they need it. Its format ranges from ebooks and enhanced ebooks to mobile apps and print books available through print-on-demand technology. Directed to a general business audience, the Press's areas of interest include management and strategy, innovation and entrepreneurship, finance and investment, leadership, marketing, operations, human resources, social responsibility, business-government relations, and more.

wdp.wharton.upenn.edu

Wharton
UNIVERSITY *of* PENNSYLVANIA

About The Wharton School

The Wharton School of the University of Pennsylvania—founded in 1881 as the first collegiate business school—is recognized globally for intellectual leadership and ongoing innovation across every major discipline of business education. The most comprehensive source of business knowledge in the world, Wharton bridges research and practice through its broad engagement with the global business community. The School has more than 4,800 undergraduate, MBA, executive MBA, and doctoral students; more than 9,000 annual participants in executive education programs; and an alumni network of 86,000 graduates.

www.wharton.upenn.edu